AI
Autonomous Cars
Progress

Practical Advances in
Artificial Intelligence and Machine Learning

Dr. Lance B. Eliot, MBA, PhD

DEDICATION

To my incredible daughter, Lauren, and my incredible son, Michael.

Forest fortuna adiuvat (from the Latin; good fortune favors the brave).

CONTENTS

Lance B. Eliot

ACKNOWLEDGMENTS

I have been the beneficiary of advice and counsel by many friends, colleagues, family, investors, and many others. I want to thank everyone that has aided me throughout my career. I write from the heart and the head, having experienced first-hand what it means to have others around you that support you during the good times and the tough times.

To Warren Bennis, one of my doctoral advisors and ultimately a colleague, I offer my deepest thanks and appreciation, especially for his calm and insightful wisdom and support.

To Mark Stevens and his generous efforts toward funding and supporting the USC Stevens Center for Innovation.

To Lloyd Greif and the USC Lloyd Greif Center for Entrepreneurial Studies for their ongoing encouragement of founders and entrepreneurs.

To Peter Drucker, William Wang, Aaron Levie, Peter Kim, Jon Kraft, Cindy Crawford, Jenny Ming, Steve Milligan, Chis Underwood, Frank Gehry, Buzz Aldrin, Steve Forbes, Bill Thompson, Dave Dillon, Alan Fuerstman, Larry Ellison, Jim Sinegal, John Sperling, Mark Stevenson, Anand Nallathambi, Thomas Barrack, Jr., and many other innovators and leaders that I have met and gained mightily from doing so.

Thanks to Ed Trainor, Kevin Anderson, James Hickey, Wendell Jones, Ken Harris, DuWayne Peterson, Mike Brown, Jim Thornton, Abhi Beniwal, Al Biland, John Nomura, Eliot Weinman, John Desmond, and many others for their unwavering support during my career.

And most of all thanks as always to Lauren and Michael, for their ongoing support and for having seen me writing and heard much of this material during the many months involved in writing it. To their patience and willingness to listen.

INTRODUCTION

This is a book that provides the newest innovations and the latest Artificial Intelligence (AI) advances about the emerging nature of AI-based autonomous self-driving driverless cars. Via recent advances in Artificial Intelligence (AI) and Machine Learning (ML), we are nearing the day when vehicles can control themselves and will not require and nor rely upon human intervention to perform their driving tasks (or, that <u>allow</u> for human intervention, but only *require* human intervention in very limited ways).

Similar to my other related books, which I describe in a moment and list the chapters in the Appendix A of this book, I am particularly focused on those advances that pertain to self-driving cars. The phrase "autonomous vehicles" is often used to refer to any kind of vehicle, whether it is ground-based or in the air or sea, and whether it is a cargo hauling trailer truck or a conventional passenger car. Though the aspects described in this book are certainly applicable to all kinds of autonomous vehicles, I am focused more so here on cars.

Indeed, I am especially known for my role in aiding the advancement of self-driving cars, serving currently as the Executive Director of the Cybernetic AI Self-Driving Cars Institute.. In addition to writing software, designing and developing systems and software for self-driving cars, I also speak and write quite a bit about the topic. This book is a collection of some of my more advanced essays. For those of you that might have seen my essays posted elsewhere, I have updated them and integrated them into this book as one handy cohesive package.

You might be interested in companion books that I have written that provide additional key innovations and fundamentals about self-driving cars. Those books are entitled **"Introduction to Driverless Self-Driving Cars," "Advances in AI and Autonomous Vehicles: Cybernetic Self-Driving Cars," "Self-Driving Cars: "The Mother of All AI Projects," "Innovation and Thought Leadership on Self-Driving Driverless Cars," "New Advances in AI Autonomous Driverless Self-Driving Cars," "Autonomous Vehicle Driverless Self-Driving Cars and Artificial Intelligence," "Transformative Artificial Intelligence**

1

Driverless Self-Driving Cars," "Disruptive Artificial Intelligence and Driverless Self-Driving Cars, and "State-of-the-Art AI Driverless Self-Driving Cars," and "Top Trends in AI Self-Driving Cars," and "AI Innovations and Self-Driving Cars," "Crucial Advances for AI Driverless Cars," "Sociotechnical Insights and AI Driverless Cars," "Pioneering Advances for AI Driverless Cars" and "Leading Edge Trends for AI Driverless Cars," "The Cutting Edge of AI Autonomous Cars" and "The Next Wave of AI Self-Driving Cars" and "Revolutionary Innovations of AI Self-Driving Cars," and "AI Self-Driving Cars Breakthroughs," "Trailblazing Trends for AI Self-Driving Cars," "Ingenious Strides for AI Driverless Cars," "AI Self-Driving Cars Inventiveness," "Visionary Secrets of AI Driverless Cars," "Spearheading AI Self-Driving Cars," "Spurring AI Self-Driving Cars," "Avant-Garde AI Driverless Cars," "AI Self-Driving Cars Evolvement," "AI Driverless Cars Chrysalis," "Boosting AI Autonomous Cars," "AI Self-Driving Cars Trendsetting," and "AI Autonomous Cars Forefront, "AI Autonomous Cars Emergence," "AI Autonomous Cars Progress" (they are all available via Amazon). Appendix A has a listing of the chapters covered.

For this book, I am going to borrow my introduction from those companion books, since it does a good job of laying out the landscape of self-driving cars and my overall viewpoints on the topic. The remainder of this book is material that does not appear in the companion books.

INTRODUCTION TO SELF-DRIVING CARS

This is a book about self-driving cars. Someday in the future, we'll all have self-driving cars and this book will perhaps seem antiquated, but right now, we are at the forefront of the self-driving car wave. Daily news bombards us with flashes of new announcements by one car maker or another and leaves the impression that within the next few weeks or maybe months that the self-driving car will be here. A casual non-technical reader would assume from these news flashes that in fact we must be on the cusp of a true self-driving car. Here's a real news flash: We are still quite a distance from having a true self-driving car. It is years to go before we get there.

Why is that? Because a true self-driving car is akin to a moonshot. In the same manner that getting us to the moon was an incredible feat, likewise is achieving a true self-driving car. Anybody that suggests or even brashly states that the true self-driving car is nearly here should be viewed with great skepticism. Indeed, you'll see that I often tend to use the word "hogwash" or "crock" when I assess much of the decidedly *fake news* about self-driving cars.

Indeed, I've been writing a popular blog post about self-driving cars and hitting hard on those that try to wave their hands and pretend that we are on the imminent verge of true self-driving cars. For many years, I've been known as the AI Insider. Besides writing about AI, I also develop AI software. I do what I describe. It also gives me insights into what others that are doing AI are really doing versus what it is said they are doing.

Many faithful readers had asked me to pull together my insightful short essays and put them into another book, which you are now holding.

For those of you that have been reading my essays over the years, this collection not only puts them together into one handy package, I also updated the essays and added new material. For those of you that are new to the topic of self-driving cars and AI, I hope you find these essays approachable and informative. I also tend to have a writing style with a bit of a voice, and so you'll see that I am times have a wry sense of humor and poke at conformity.

As a former professor and founder of an AI research lab, I for many years wrote in the formal language of academic writing. I published in referred journals and served as an editor for several AI journals. This writing here is not of the nature, and I have adopted a different and more informal style for these essays. That being said, I also do mention from time-to-time more rigorous material on AI and encourage you all to dig into those deeper and more formal materials if so interested.

I am also an AI practitioner. This means that I write AI software for a living. Currently, I head-up the Cybernetics Self-Driving Car Institute, where we are developing AI software for self-driving cars. I am excited to also report that my son, also a software engineer, heads-up our Cybernetics Self-Driving Car Lab. What I have helped to start, and for which he is an integral part, ultimately he will carry long into the future after I have retired. My daughter, a marketing whiz, also is integral to our efforts as head of our Marketing group. She too will carry forward the legacy now being formulated.

For those of you that are reading this book and have a penchant for writing code, you might consider taking a look at the open source code available for self-driving cars. This is a handy place to start learning how to develop AI for self-driving cars. There are also many new educational courses spring forth. There is a growing body of those wanting to learn about and develop self-driving cars, and a growing body of colleges, labs, and other avenues by which you can learn about self-driving cars.

This book will provide a foundation of aspects that I think will get you ready for those kinds of more advanced training opportunities. If you've already taken those classes, you'll likely find these essays especially interesting as they offer a perspective that I am betting few other instructors or faculty offered to you. These are challenging essays that ask you to think beyond the conventional about self-driving cars.

THE MOTHER OF ALL AI PROJECTS

In June 2017, Apple CEO Tim Cook came out and finally admitted that Apple has been working on a self-driving car. As you'll see in my essays, Apple was enmeshed in secrecy about their self-driving car efforts. We have only been able to read the tea leaves and guess at what Apple has been up to. The notion of an iCar has been floating for quite a while, and self-driving engineers and researchers have been signing tight-lipped Non-Disclosure Agreements (NDA's) to work on projects at Apple that were as shrouded in mystery as any military invasion plans might be.

Tim Cook said something that many others in the Artificial Intelligence (AI) field have been saying, namely, the creation of a self-driving car has got to be the mother of all AI projects. In other words, it is in fact a tremendous moonshot for AI. If a self-driving car can be crafted and the AI works as we hope, it means that we have made incredible strides with AI and that therefore it opens many other worlds of potential breakthrough accomplishments that AI can solve.

Is this hyperbole? Am I just trying to make AI seem like a miracle worker and so provide self-aggrandizing statements for those of us writing the AI software for self-driving cars? No, it is not hyperbole. Developing a true self-driving car is really, really, really hard to do. Let me take a moment to explain why. As a side note, I realize that the Apple CEO is known for at times uttering hyperbole, and he had previously said for example that the year 2012 was "the mother of all years," and he had said that the release of iOS 10 was "the mother of all releases" – all of which does suggest he likes to use the handy "mother of" expression. But, I assure you, in terms of true self-driving cars, he has hit the nail on the head. For sure.

When you think about a moonshot and how we got to the moon, there are some identifiable characteristics and those same aspects can be applied to creating a true self-driving car. You'll notice that I keep putting the word "true" in front of the self-driving car expression. I do so because as per my essay about the various levels of self-driving cars, there are some self-driving cars that are only somewhat of a self-driving car. The somewhat versions are ones that require a human driver to be ready to intervene. In my view, that's not a true self-driving car. A true self-driving car is one that requires no human driver intervention at all. It is a car that can entirely undertake via automation the driving task without any human driver needed. This is the essence of what is known as a Level 5 self-driving car. We are currently at the Level 2 and Level 3 mark, and not yet at Level 5.

Getting to the moon involved aspects such as having big stretch goals, incremental progress, experimentation, innovation, and so on. Let's review how this applied to the moonshot of the bygone era, and how it applies to the self-driving car moonshot of today.

Big Stretch Goal

Trying to take a human and deliver the human to the moon, and bring them back, safely, was an extremely large stretch goal at the time. No one knew whether it could be done. The technology wasn't available yet. The cost was huge. The determination would need to be fierce. Etc. To reach a Level 5 self-driving car is going to be the same. It is a big stretch goal. We can readily get to the Level 3, and we are able to see the Level 4 just up ahead, but a Level 5 is still an unknown as to if it is doable. It should eventually be doable and in the same way that we thought we'd eventually get to the moon, but when it will occur is a different story.

Incremental Progress

Getting to the moon did not happen overnight in one fell swoop. It took years and years of incremental progress to get there. Likewise for self-driving cars. Google has famously been striving to get to the Level 5, and pretty much been willing to forgo dealing with the intervening levels, but most of the other self-driving car makers are doing the incremental route. Let's get a good Level 2 and a somewhat Level 3 going. Then, let's improve the Level 3 and get a somewhat Level 4 going. Then, let's improve the Level 4 and finally arrive at a Level 5. This seems to be the prevalent way that we are going to achieve the true self-driving car.

Experimentation

You likely know that there were various experiments involved in perfecting the approach and technology to get to the moon. As per making incremental progress, we first tried to see if we could get a rocket to go into space and safety return, then put a monkey in there, then with a human, then we went all the way to the moon but didn't land, and finally we arrived at the mission that actually landed on the moon. Self-driving cars are the same way. We are doing simulations of self-driving cars. We do testing of self-driving cars on private land under controlled situations. We do testing of self-driving cars on public roadways, often having to meet regulatory requirements including for example having an engineer or equivalent in the car to take over the controls if needed. And so on. Experiments big and small are needed to figure out what works and what doesn't.

Innovation

There are already some advances in AI that are allowing us to progress toward self-driving cars. We are going to need even more advances. Innovation in all aspects of technology are going to be required to achieve a true self-driving car. By no means do we already have everything in-hand that we need to get there. Expect new inventions and new approaches, new algorithms, etc.

Setbacks

Most of the pundits are avoiding talking about potential setbacks in the progress toward self-driving cars. Getting to the moon involved many setbacks, some of which you never have heard of and were buried at the time so as to not dampen enthusiasm and funding for getting to the moon. A recurring theme in many of my included essays is that there are going to be setbacks as we try to arrive at a true self-driving car. Take a deep breath and be ready. I just hope the setbacks don't completely stop progress. I am sure that it will cause progress to alter in a manner that we've not yet seen in the self-driving car field. I liken the self-driving car of today to the excitement everyone had for Uber when it first got going. Today, we have a different view of Uber and with each passing day there are more regulations to the ride sharing business and more concerns raised. The darling child only stays a darling until finally that child acts up. It will happen the same with self-driving cars.

SELF-DRIVING CARS CHALLENGES

But what exactly makes things so hard to have a true self-driving car, you might be asking. You have seen cruise control for years and years. You've lately seen cars that can do parallel parking. You've seen YouTube videos of Tesla drivers that put their hands out the window as their car zooms along the highway, and seen to therefore be in a self-driving car. Aren't we just needing to put a few more sensors onto a car and then we'll have in-hand a true self-driving car? Nope.

Consider for a moment the nature of the driving task. We don't just let anyone at any age drive a car. Worldwide, most countries won't license a driver until the age of 18, though many do allow a learner's permit at the age of 15 or 16. Some suggest that a younger age would be physically too small to reach the controls of the car. Though this might be the case, we could easily adjust the controls to allow for younger aged and thus smaller stature. It's not their physical size that matters. It's their cognitive development that matters.

To drive a car, you need to be able to reason about the car, what the car can and cannot do. You need to know how to operate the car. You need to know about how other cars on the road drive. You need to know what is allowed in driving such as speed limits and driving within marked lanes. You need to be able to react to situations and be able to avoid getting into accidents. You need to ascertain when to hit your brakes, when to steer clear of a pedestrian, and how to keep from ramming that motorcyclist that just cut you off.

Many of us had taken courses on driving. We studied about driving and took driver training. We had to take a test and pass it to be able to drive. The point being that though most adults take the driving task for granted, and we often "mindlessly" drive our cars, there is a significant amount of cognitive effort that goes into driving a car. After a while, it becomes second nature. You don't especially think about how you drive, you just do it. But, if you watch a novice driver, say a teenager learning to drive, you suddenly realize that there is a lot more complexity to it than we seem to realize.

Furthermore, driving is a very serious task. I recall when my daughter and son first learned to drive. They are both very conscientious people. They wanted to make sure that whatever they did, they did well, and that they did not harm anyone. Every day, when you get into a car, it is probably around 4,000 pounds of hefty metal and plastics (about two tons), and it is a lethal weapon. Think about it. You drive down the street in an object that weighs two tons and with the engine it can accelerate and ram into anything you want to hit. The damage a car can inflict is very scary. Both my children were surprised that they were being given the right to maneuver this monster of a beast that could cause tremendous harm entirely by merely letting go of the steering wheel for a moment or taking your eyes off the road.

In fact, in the United States alone there are about 30,000 deaths per year by auto accidents, which is around 100 per day. Given that there are about 263 million cars in the United States, I am actually more amazed that the number of fatalities is not a lot higher. During my morning commute, I look at all the thousands of cars on the freeway around me, and I think that if all of them decided to go zombie and drive in a crazy maniac way, there would be many people dead. Somehow, incredibly, each day, most people drive relatively safely. To me, that's a miracle right there. Getting millions and millions of people to be safe and sane when behind the wheel of a two ton mobile object, it's a feat that we as a society should admire with pride.

So, hopefully you are in agreement that the driving task requires a great deal of cognition. You don't' need to be especially smart to drive a car, and we've done quite a bit to make car driving viable for even the average dolt. There isn't an IQ test that you need to take to drive a car. If you can read and write, and pass a test, you pretty much can legally drive a car. There are of course some that drive a car and are not legally permitted to do so, plus there are private areas such as farms where drivers are young, but for public roadways in the United States, you can be generally of average intelligence (or less) and be able to legally drive.

This though makes it seem like the cognitive effort must not be much. If the cognitive effort was truly hard, wouldn't we only have Einstein's that could drive a car? We have made sure to keep the driving task as simple as we can, by making the controls easy and relatively standardized, and by having roads that are relatively standardized, and so on. It is as though Disneyland has put their Autopia into the real-world, by us all as a society agreeing that roads will be a certain way, and we'll all abide by the various rules of driving.

A modest cognitive task by a human is still something that stymies AI. You certainly know that AI has been able to beat chess players and be good at other kinds of games. This type of narrow cognition is not what car driving is about. Car driving is much wider. It requires knowledge about the world, which a chess playing AI system does not need to know. The cognitive aspects of driving are on the one hand seemingly simple, but at the same time require layer upon layer of knowledge about cars, people, roads, rules, and a myriad of other "common sense" aspects. We don't have any AI systems today that have that same kind of breadth and depth of awareness and knowledge.

As revealed in my essays, the self-driving car of today is using trickery to do particular tasks. It is all very narrow in operation. Plus, it currently assumes that a human driver is ready to intervene. It is like a child that we have taught to stack blocks, but we are needed to be right there in case the child stacks them too high and they begin to fall over. AI of today is brittle, it is narrow, and it does not approach the cognitive abilities of humans. This is why the true self-driving car is somewhere out in the future.

Another aspect to the driving task is that it is not solely a mind exercise. You do need to use your senses to drive. You use your eyes a vision sensors to see the road ahead. You vision capability is like a streaming video, which your brain needs to continually analyze as you drive. Where is the road? Is there a pedestrian in the way? Is there another car ahead of you? Your senses are relying a flood of info to your brain. Self-driving cars are trying to do the same, by using cameras, radar, ultrasound, and lasers. This is an attempt at mimicking how humans have senses and sensory apparatus.

Thus, the driving task is mental and physical. You use your senses, you use your arms and legs to manipulate the controls of the car, and you use your brain to assess the sensory info and direct your limbs to act upon the controls of the car. This all happens instantly. If you've ever perhaps gotten something in your eye and only had one eye available to drive with, you suddenly realize how dependent upon vision you are. If you have a broken foot with a cast, you suddenly realize how hard it is to control the brake pedal and the accelerator. If you've taken medication and your brain is maybe sluggish, you suddenly realize how much mental strain is required to drive a car.

An AI system that plays chess only needs to be focused on playing chess. The physical aspects aren't important because usually a human moves the chess pieces or the chessboard is shown on an electronic display. Using AI for a more life-and-death task such as analyzing MRI images of patients, this again does not require physical capabilities and instead is done by examining images of bits.

Driving a car is a true life-and-death task. It is a use of AI that can easily and at any moment produce death. For those colleagues of mine that are developing this AI, as am I, we need to keep in mind the somber aspects of this. We are producing software that will have in its virtual hands the lives of the occupants of the car, and the lives of those in other nearby cars, and the lives of nearby pedestrians, etc. Chess is not usually a life-or-death matter.

Driving is all around us. Cars are everywhere. Most of today's AI applications involve only a small number of people. Or, they are behind the scenes and we as humans have other recourse if the AI messes up. AI that is driving a car at 80 miles per hour on a highway had better not mess up. The consequences are grave. Multiply this by the number of cars, if we could put magically self-driving into every car in the USA, we'd have AI running in the 263 million cars. That's a lot of AI spread around. This is AI on a massive scale that we are not doing today and that offers both promise and potential peril.

There are some that want AI for self-driving cars because they envision a world without any car accidents. They envision a world in which there is no car congestion and all cars cooperate with each other. These are wonderful utopian visions.

They are also very misleading. The adoption of self-driving cars is going to be incremental and not overnight. We cannot economically just junk all existing cars. Nor are we going to be able to affordably retrofit existing cars. It is more likely that self-driving cars will be built into new cars and that over many years of gradual replacement of existing cars that we'll see the mix of self-driving cars become substantial in the real-world.

In these essays, I have tried to offer technological insights without being overly technical in my description, and also blended the business, societal, and economic aspects too. Technologists need to consider the non-technological impacts of what they do. Non-technologists should be aware of what is being developed.

We all need to work together to collectively be prepared for the enormous disruption and transformative aspects of true self-driving cars. We all need to be involved in this mother of all AI projects.

WHAT THIS BOOK PROVIDES

What does this book provide to you? It introduces many of the key elements about self-driving cars and does so with an AI based perspective. I weave together technical and non-technical aspects, readily going from being concerned about the cognitive capabilities of the driving task and how the technology is embodying this into self-driving cars, and in the next breath I discuss the societal and economic aspects.

They are all intertwined because that's the way reality is. You cannot separate out the technology per se, and instead must consider it within the milieu of what is being invented and innovated, and do so with a mindset towards the contemporary mores and culture that shape what we are doing and what we hope to do.

WHY THIS BOOK

I wrote this book to try and bring to the public view many aspects about self-driving cars that nobody seems to be discussing.

For business leaders that are either involved in making self-driving cars or that are going to leverage self-driving cars, I hope that this book will enlighten you as to the risks involved and ways in which you should be strategizing about how to deal with those risks.

For entrepreneurs, startups and other businesses that want to enter into the self-driving car market that is emerging, I hope this book sparks your interest in doing so, and provides some sense of what might be prudent to pursue.

For researchers that study self-driving cars, I hope this book spurs your interest in the risks and safety issues of self-driving cars, and also nudges you toward conducting research on those aspects.

For students in computer science or related disciplines, I hope this book will provide you with interesting and new ideas and material, for which you might conduct research or provide some career direction insights for you.

For AI companies and high-tech companies pursuing self-driving cars, this book will hopefully broaden your view beyond just the mere coding and development needed to make self-driving cars.

For all readers, I hope that you will find the material in this book to be stimulating. Some of it will be repetitive of things you already know. But I am pretty sure that you'll also find various eureka moments whereby you'll discover a new technique or approach that you had not earlier thought of. I am also betting that there will be material that forces you to rethink some of your current practices.

I am not saying you will suddenly have an epiphany and change what you are doing. I do think though that you will reconsider or perhaps revisit what you are doing.

For anyone choosing to use this book for teaching purposes, please take a look at my suggestions for doing so, as described in the Appendix. I have found the material handy in courses that I have taught, and likewise other faculty have told me that they have found the material handy, in some cases as extended readings and in other instances as a core part of their course (depending on the nature of the class).

In my writing for this book, I have tried carefully to blend both the practitioner and the academic styles of writing. It is not as dense as is typical academic journal writing, but at the same time offers depth by going into the nuances and trade-offs of various practices.

The word "deep" is in vogue today, meaning getting deeply into a subject or topic, and so is the word "unpack" which means to tease out the underlying aspects of a subject or topic. I have sought to offer material that addresses an issue or topic by going relatively deeply into it and make sure that it is well unpacked.

In any book about AI, it is difficult to use our everyday words without having some of them be misinterpreted. Specifically, it is easy to anthropomorphize AI. When I say that an AI system "knows" something, I do not want you to construe that the AI system has sentience and "knows" in the same way that humans do. They aren't that way, as yet. I have tried to use quotes around such words from time-to-time to emphasize that the words I am using should not be misinterpreted to ascribe true human intelligence to the AI systems that we know of today. If I used quotes around all such words, the book would be very difficult to read, and so I am doing so judiciously. Please keep that in mind as you read the material, thanks.

Some of the material is time-based in terms of covering underway activities, and though some of it might decay, nonetheless I believe you'll find the material useful and informative.

COMPANION BOOKS

1. **"Introduction to Driverless Self-Driving Cars"** by Dr. Lance Eliot
2. **"Innovation and Thought Leadership on Self-Driving Driverless Cars"** by Dr. Lance Eliot
3. **"Advances in AI and Autonomous Vehicles: Cybernetic Self-Driving Cars"** by Dr. Lance Eliot
4. **"Self-Driving Cars: The Mother of All AI Projects"** by Dr. Lance Eliot
5. **"New Advances in AI Autonomous Driverless Self-Driving Cars"** by Dr. Lance Eliot
6. **"Autonomous Vehicle Driverless Self-Driving Cars and Artificial Intelligence"** by Dr. Lance Eliot and Michael B. Eliot
7. **"Transformative Artificial Intelligence Driverless Self-Driving Cars"** by Dr. Lance Eliot
8. **"Disruptive Artificial Intelligence and Driverless Self-Driving Cars"** by Dr. Lance Eliot
9. "State-of-the-Art AI Driverless Self-Driving Cars" by Dr. Lance Eliot
10. **"Top Trends in AI Self-Driving Cars"** by Dr. Lance Eliot
11. **"AI Innovations and Self-Driving Cars"** by Dr. Lance Eliot
12. **"Crucial Advances for AI Driverless Cars"** by Dr. Lance Eliot
13. **"Sociotechnical Insights and AI Driverless Cars"** by Dr. Lance Eliot.
14. **"Pioneering Advances for AI Driverless Cars"** by Dr. Lance Eliot
15. **"Leading Edge Trends for AI Driverless Cars"** by Dr. Lance Eliot
16. **"The Cutting Edge of AI Autonomous Cars"** by Dr. Lance Eliot
17. **"The Next Wave of AI Self-Driving Cars"** by Dr. Lance Eliot
18. **"Revolutionary Innovations of AI Driverless Cars"** by Dr. Lance Eliot
19. **"AI Self-Driving Cars Breakthroughs"** by Dr. Lance Eliot
20. **"Trailblazing Trends for AI Self-Driving Cars"** by Dr. Lance Eliot
21. **"Ingenious Strides for AI Driverless Cars"** by Dr. Lance Eliot
22. **"AI Self-Driving Cars Inventiveness"** by Dr. Lance Eliot
23. **"Visionary Secrets of AI Driverless Cars"** by Dr. Lance Eliot
24. **"Spearheading AI Self-Driving Cars"** by Dr. Lance Eliot
25. **"Spurring AI Self-Driving Cars"** by Dr. Lance Eliot
26. **"Avant-Garde AI Driverless Cars"** by Dr. Lance Eliot
27. **"AI Self-Driving Cars Evolvement"** by Dr. Lance Eliot
28. **"AI Driverless Cars Chrysalis"** by Dr. Lance Eliot
29. **"Boosting AI Autonomous Cars"** by Dr. Lance Eliot
30. **"AI Self-Driving Cars Trendsetting"** by Dr. Lance Eliot
31. **"AI Autonomous Cars Forefront"** by Dr. Lance Eliot
32. **"AI Autonomous Cars Emergence"** by Dr. Lance Eliot
33. **"AI Autonomous Cars Progress"** by Dr. Lance Eliot

These books are available on Amazon and at other major global booksellers.

CHAPTER 1

ELIOT FRAMEWORK FOR AI SELF-DRIVING CARS

CHAPTER 1

ELIOT FRAMEWORK FOR AI SELF-DRIVING CARS

This chapter is a core foundational aspect for understanding AI self-driving cars and I have used this same chapter in several of my other books to introduce the reader to essential elements of this field. Once you've read this chapter, you'll be prepared to read the rest of the material since the foundational essence of the components of autonomous AI driverless self-driving cars will have been established for you.

When I give presentations about self-driving cars and teach classes on the topic, I have found it helpful to provide a framework around which the various key elements of self-driving cars can be understood and organized (see diagram at the end of this chapter). The framework needs to be simple enough to convey the overarching elements, but at the same time not so simple that it belies the true complexity of self-driving cars. As such, I am going to describe the framework here and try to offer in a thousand words (or more!) what the framework diagram itself intends to portray.

The core elements on the diagram are numbered for ease of reference. The numbering does not suggest any kind of prioritization of the elements. Each element is crucial. Each element has a purpose, and otherwise would not be included in the framework. For some self-driving cars, a particular element might be more important or somehow distinguished in comparison to other self-driving cars.

You could even use the framework to rate a particular self-driving car, doing so by gauging how well it performs in each of the elements of the framework. I will describe each of the elements, one at a time. After doing so, I'll discuss aspects that illustrate how the elements interact and perform during the overall effort of a self-driving car.

At the Cybernetic Self-Driving Car Institute, we use the framework to keep track of what we are working on, and how we are developing software that fills in what is needed to achieve Level 5 self-driving cars.

D-01: Sensor Capture

Let's start with the one element that often gets the most attention in the press about self-driving cars, namely, the sensory devices for a self-driving car.

On the framework, the box labeled as D-01 indicates "Sensor Capture" and refers to the processes of the self-driving car that involve collecting data from the myriad of sensors that are used for a self-driving car. The types of devices typically involved are listed, such as the use of mono cameras, stereo cameras, LIDAR devices, radar systems, ultrasonic devices, GPS, IMU, and so on.

These devices are tasked with obtaining data about the status of the self-driving car and the world around it. Some of the devices are continually providing updates, while others of the devices await an indication by the self-driving car that the device is supposed to collect data. The data might be first transformed in some fashion by the device itself, or it might instead be fed directly into the sensor capture as raw data. At that point, it might be up to the sensor capture processes to do transformations on the data. This all varies depending upon the nature of the devices being used and how the devices were designed and developed.

D-02: Sensor Fusion

Imagine that your eyeballs receive visual images, your nose receives odors, your ears receive sounds, and in essence each of your distinct sensory devices is getting some form of input. The input befits the nature of the device. Likewise, for a self-driving car, the cameras provide visual images, the radar returns radar reflections, and so on.

Each device provides the data as befits what the device does.

At some point, using the analogy to humans, you need to merge together what your eyes see, what your nose smells, what your ears hear, and piece it all together into a larger sense of what the world is all about and what is happening around you. Sensor fusion is the action of taking the singular aspects from each of the devices and putting them together into a larger puzzle.

Sensor fusion is a tough task. There are some devices that might not be working at the time of the sensor capture. Or, there might some devices that are unable to report well what they have detected. Again, using a human analogy, suppose you are in a dark room and so your eyes cannot see much. At that point, you might need to rely more so on your ears and what you hear. The same is true for a self-driving car. If the cameras are obscured due to snow and sleet, it might be that the radar can provide a greater indication of what the external conditions consist of.

In the case of a self-driving car, there can be a plethora of such sensory devices. Each is reporting what it can. Each might have its difficulties. Each might have its limitations, such as how far ahead it can detect an object. All of these limitations need to be considered during the sensor fusion task.

D-03: Virtual World Model

For humans, we presumably keep in our minds a model of the world around us when we are driving a car. In your mind, you know that the car is going at say 60 miles per hour and that you are on a freeway. You have a model in your mind that your car is surrounded by other cars, and that there are lanes to the freeway. Your model is not only based on what you can see, hear, etc., but also what you know about the nature of the world. You know that at any moment that car ahead of you can smash on its brakes, or the car behind you can ram into your car, or that the truck in the next lane might swerve into your lane.

The AI of the self-driving car needs to have a virtual world model, which it then keeps updated with whatever it is receiving from the sensor fusion, which received its input from the sensor capture and the sensory devices.

D-04: System Action Plan

By having a virtual world model, the AI of the self-driving car is able to keep track of where the car is and what is happening around the car. In addition, the AI needs to determine what to do next. Should the self-driving car hit its brakes? Should the self-driving car stay in its lane or swerve into the lane to the left? Should the self-driving car accelerate or slow down?

A system action plan needs to be prepared by the AI of the self-driving car. The action plan specifies what actions should be taken. The actions need to pertain to the status of the virtual world model. Plus, the actions need to be realizable.

This realizability means that the AI cannot just assert that the self-driving car should suddenly sprout wings and fly. Instead, the AI must be bound by whatever the self-driving car can actually do, such as coming to a halt in a distance of X feet at a speed of Y miles per hour, rather than perhaps asserting that the self-driving car come to a halt in 0 feet as though it could instantaneously come to a stop while it is in motion.

D-05: Controls Activation

The system action plan is implemented by activating the controls of the car to act according to what the plan stipulates. This might mean that the accelerator control is commanded to increase the speed of the car. Or, the steering control is commanded to turn the steering wheel 30 degrees to the left or right.

One question arises as to whether or not the controls respond as they are commanded to do. In other words, suppose the AI has commanded the accelerator to increase, but for some reason it does not do so. Or, maybe it tries to do so, but the speed of the car does not increase. The controls activation feeds back into the virtual world model, and simultaneously the virtual world model is getting updated from the sensors, the sensor capture, and the sensor fusion. This allows the AI to ascertain what has taken place as a result of the controls being commanded to take some kind of action.

By the way, please keep in mind that though the diagram seems to have a linear progression to it, the reality is that these are all aspects of the self-driving car that are happening in parallel and simultaneously. The sensors are capturing data, meanwhile the sensor fusion is taking place, meanwhile the virtual model is being updated, meanwhile the system action plan is being formulated and reformulated, meanwhile the controls are being activated.

This is the same as a human being that is driving a car. They are eyeballing the road, meanwhile they are fusing in their mind the sights, sounds, etc., meanwhile their mind is updating their model of the world around them, meanwhile they are formulating an action plan of what to do, and meanwhile they are pushing their foot onto the pedals and steering the car. In the normal course of driving a car, you are doing all of these at once. I mention this so that when you look at the diagram, you will think of the boxes as processes that are all happening at the same time, and not as though only one happens and then the next.

They are shown diagrammatically in a simplistic manner to help comprehend what is taking place. You though should also realize that they are working in parallel and simultaneous with each other. This is a tough aspect in that the inter-element communications involve latency and other aspects that must be taken into account. There can be delays in one element updating and then sharing its latest status with other elements.

D-06: Automobile & CAN

Contemporary cars use various automotive electronics and a Controller Area Network (CAN) to serve as the components that underlie the driving aspects of a car. There are Electronic Control Units (ECU's) which control subsystems of the car, such as the engine, the brakes, the doors, the windows, and so on.

The elements D-01, D-02, D-03, D-04, D-05 are layered on top of the D-06, and must be aware of the nature of what the D-06 is able to do and not do.

D-07: In-Car Commands

Humans are going to be occupants in self-driving cars. In a Level 5 self-driving car, there must be some form of communication that takes place between the humans and the self-driving car. For example, I go into a self-driving car and tell it that I want to be driven over to Disneyland, and along the way I want to stop at In-and-Out Burger. The self-driving car now parses what I've said and tries to then establish a means to carry out my wishes.

In-car commands can happen at any time during a driving journey. Though my example was about an in-car command when I first got into my self-driving car, it could be that while the self-driving car is carrying out the journey that I change my mind. Perhaps after getting stuck in traffic, I tell the self-driving car to forget about getting the burgers and just head straight over to the theme park. The self-driving car needs to be alert to in-car commands throughout the journey.

D-08: V2X Communications

We will ultimately have self-driving cars communicating with each other, doing so via V2V (Vehicle-to-Vehicle) communications. We will also have self-driving cars that communicate with the roadways and other aspects of the transportation infrastructure, doing so via V2I (Vehicle-to-Infrastructure).

The variety of ways in which a self-driving car will be communicating with other cars and infrastructure is being called V2X, whereby the letter X means whatever else we identify as something that a car should or would want to communicate with. The V2X communications will be taking place simultaneous with everything else on the diagram, and those other elements will need to incorporate whatever it gleans from those V2X communications.

D-09: Deep Learning

The use of Deep Learning permeates all other aspects of the self-driving car. The AI of the self-driving car will be using deep learning to do a better job at the systems action plan, and at the controls activation, and at the sensor fusion, and so on.

Currently, the use of artificial neural networks is the most prevalent form of deep learning. Based on large swaths of data, the neural networks attempt to "learn" from the data and therefore direct the efforts of the self-driving car accordingly.

D-10: Tactical AI

Tactical AI is the element of dealing with the moment-to-moment driving of the self-driving car. Is the self-driving car staying in its lane of the freeway? Is the car responding appropriately to the controls commands? Are the sensory devices working?

For human drivers, the tactical equivalent can be seen when you watch a novice driver such as a teenager that is first driving. They are focused on the mechanics of the driving task, keeping their eye on the road while also trying to properly control the car.

D-11: Strategic AI

The Strategic AI aspects of a self-driving car are dealing with the larger picture of what the self-driving car is trying to do. If I had asked that the self-driving car take me to Disneyland, there is an overall journey map that needs to be kept and maintained.

There is an interaction between the Strategic AI and the Tactical AI. The Strategic AI is wanting to keep on the mission of the driving, while the Tactical AI is focused on the particulars underway in the driving effort. If the Tactical AI seems to wander away from the overarching mission, the Strategic AI wants to see why and get things back on track. If the Tactical AI realizes that there is something amiss on the self-driving car, it needs to alert the Strategic AI accordingly and have an adjustment to the overarching mission that is underway.

D-12: Self-Aware AI

Very few of the self-driving cars being developed are including a Self-Aware AI element, which we at the Cybernetic Self-Driving Car Institute believe is crucial to Level 5 self-driving cars.

The Self-Aware AI element is intended to watch over itself, in the sense that the AI is making sure that the AI is working as intended. Suppose you had a human driving a car, and they were starting to drive erratically. Hopefully, their own self-awareness would make them realize they themselves are driving poorly, such as perhaps starting to fall asleep after having been driving for hours on end. If you had a passenger in the car, they might be able to alert the driver if the driver is starting to do something amiss. This is exactly what the Self-Aware

AI element tries to do, it becomes the overseer of the AI, and tries to detect when the AI has become faulty or confused, and then find ways to overcome the issue.

D-13: Economic

The economic aspects of a self-driving car are not per se a technology aspect of a self-driving car, but the economics do indeed impact the nature of a self-driving car. For example, the cost of outfitting a self-driving car with every kind of possible sensory device is prohibitive, and so choices need to be made about which devices are used. And, for those sensory devices chosen, whether they would have a full set of features or a more limited set of features.

We are going to have self-driving cars that are at the low-end of a consumer cost point, and others at the high-end of a consumer cost point. You cannot expect that the self-driving car at the low-end is going to be as robust as the one at the high-end. I realize that many of the self-driving car pundits are acting as though all self-driving cars will be the same, but they won't be. Just like anything else, we are going to have self-driving cars that have a range of capabilities. Some will be better than others. Some will be safer than others. This is the way of the real-world, and so we need to be thinking about the economics aspects when considering the nature of self-driving cars.

D-14: Societal

This component encompasses the societal aspects of AI which also impacts the technology of self-driving cars. For example, the famous Trolley Problem involves what choices should a self-driving car make when faced with life-and-death matters. If the self-driving car is about to either hit a child standing in the roadway, or instead ram into a tree at the side of the road and possibly kill the humans in the self-driving car, which choice should be made?

We need to keep in mind the societal aspects will underlie the AI of the self-driving car. Whether we are aware of it explicitly or not, the AI will have embedded into it various societal assumptions.

D-15: Innovation

I included the notion of innovation into the framework because we can anticipate that whatever a self-driving car consists of, it will continue to be innovated over time. The self-driving cars coming out in the next several years will undoubtedly be different and less innovative than the versions that come out in ten years hence, and so on.

Framework Overall

For those of you that want to learn about self-driving cars, you can potentially pick a particular element and become specialized in that aspect. Some engineers are focusing on the sensory devices. Some engineers focus on the controls activation. And so on. There are specialties in each of the elements.

Researchers are likewise specializing in various aspects. For example, there are researchers that are using Deep Learning to see how best it can be used for sensor fusion. There are other researchers that are using Deep Learning to derive good System Action Plans. Some are studying how to develop AI for the Strategic aspects of the driving task, while others are focused on the Tactical aspects.

A well-prepared all-around software developer that is involved in self-driving cars should be familiar with all of the elements, at least to the degree that they know what each element does. This is important since whatever piece of the pie that the software developer works on, they need to be knowledgeable about what the other elements are doing.

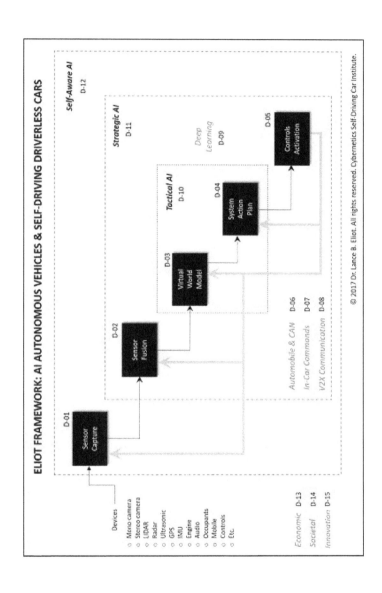

ELIOT FRAMEWORK: AI AUTONOMOUS VEHICLES & SELF-DRIVING DRIVERLESS CARS

CHAPTER 2
RISK-O-METERS
AND
AI SELF-DRIVING CARS

Lance B. Eliot

CHAPTER 2

RISK-O-METERS
AND AI SELF-DRIVING CARS

You are a finely tuned risk calculator.

That's right, when you are driving a car, you are in real-time having to figure out the risks of that pedestrian suddenly darting into the street, or the car ahead of you unexpectedly slamming on its brakes, or having to ascertain the odds that the cute kitty cat at the corner might inexplicably wander into the roadway in front of your car (don't hit the feline, please!).

What makes this a particularly hard-mental exercise is that you are trying to predict the future.

Most of the time, you don't know for sure that the pedestrian is going to foolishly leap in your path, and instead you need to use clues to guess at what might happen. Does the person seem poised to enter into the street and are they perhaps not paying attention to the traffic? If the person doesn't make eye contact with you, while you are driving, you can't be absolutely sure that they understand the gravity of the situation.

Think about the dozens, maybe hundreds, sometimes even thousands of off-the-cuff risk assessments you make during a driving journey.

I commute to work in Los Angeles traffic and use a variety of freeways and local streets to do so. As such, I encounter numerous instances of maniac cars around me, bicyclists nearby, motorcyclists weaving throughout traffic, adult pedestrians, young kids darting onto streets, dogs and cats, along with debris falling ahead of me such as the other day a pick-up truck dropped several cans of paint onto the road in front of me (my car ended-up with white paint splattered across the underbody, which I suppose is like getting a "free" paint job, lucky me).

You likely aren't even explicitly aware of how much risk calculating you do, but it's happening constantly while at the steering wheel.

If you observe a novice teenage driver, you can oftentimes see the expressions and contortions on their face as they are trying to piece together a complex calculus of what is going on around them.

In helping my own children to drive, they sometimes asked me whether I thought that a particular situation was going to develop. For example, a gaggle of kids walking on the sidewalk that were moving as a mass, and for which one of them was trying to urge them to all jaywalk. Would the "leader" prevail, and they might spill into the roadway, blocking traffic like a herd of cattle, or would the group resist and decide that it was better to cross at the crosswalk?

In the spur of the moment, these kinds of driving predicaments need to be analyzed, quickly, unhesitatingly, since any delay in what you do as a driver can lead to calamity.

You might be saying that you don't find yourself agonizing like this and are puzzled that I am making such a claim. Keep in mind that seasoned drivers gradually become accustomed to making those decisions, almost reflexively so, and appear to magically and seamlessly spot a situation and nearly instantaneously react. The bulk of the time we all seem to be making pretty good decisions and rendering reasonably accurate risk assessment, though of course we don't do so all of the time.

In the United States alone, there are about 6.3 million reported car crashes or accidents each year (I say "reported" since there could be even more accidents taking place and yet aren't being formally reported). Sadly, each year in the U.S. there are approximately 2.5 million injuries and 37,000 people killed due to car accidents. Much of the car crashes could have potentially been averted if the human driver was doing a better job of assessing risks and making appropriate driving choices.

Overall, it is crucial to realize that driving a car is not a black-or-white on-or-off kind of task.

There is haziness and fuzziness in the driving situations that we face. You try to make as best an evaluation of the risks involved at every moment of driving and have to live with your assessments. Sometimes you cut things pretty close and escape a bad situation by the skin of your teeth. Other times you misjudge and scrape against something or someone, or worse.

Usually, you are mentally updating the risk aspects as the driving effort is underway, such as the case of the morass of kids that might jaywalk, the leader prodding them gave up doing so, and thus the risk of them meandering out into the street was lessened. Note though that the risk did not drop to zero risk, since they could still have opted to enter into the roadway, whether randomly wandering out or because of some other factor that might prompt them to do so (say a maniacal clown appeared from behind a tree, scaring the kids into scattering onto the busy street, in spite of the oncoming car traffic, or maybe I've seen too many scary movies).

For self-driving driverless autonomous cars, one of the hardest and most vexing aspects for AI developers involves being able to craft an AI driving system that's a reliable, verifiable, robust and all-encompassing risk calculator, of which I'll inventively refer to this AI capability as a kind of risk-o-meter.

Let's unpack why a risk-o-meter is problematic to devise and field.

Risk-O-Meter Complexities Galore

Consider the wide range of factors that you take into account when trying to gauge roadway risks while driving your car.

The obvious factors include other cars, nearby scooters, bicycles, motorcycles, pogo stick riders, and other in-motion objects and artifacts. I've already mentioned the in-motion antics of pedestrians, young and old, along with the possibility of encountering dogs, cats, deer, wolves, and alligators (yes, alligators will wander onto the roads in places like Florida, as evidenced by one that did so when I took my kids to visit the theme parks in Orlando).

An in-motion object is more likely to catch your attention, though objects not yet in motion have to also be accounted for.

A tree the other day in my community decided that it was time to have a tree limb break-off and fall to the road. Someone was driving nearby the tree, doing so at the unluckiest of moments, and managed to hit the gas of the car and avoided the heavy and quite lethal tree limb.

Would you have paid any attention to a stationary and presumably static object like a tree, in terms of having to consider any risks associated with the tree while you are driving down the street?

Unless you've perchance had a tree become uprooted by a storm, I'd wager that you would not have put much cognitive effort toward assessing the risks of the tree disrupting your driving effort. This provides an example of how a seemingly motionless object can become surprisingly an impediment to driving.

Getting an AI system to do the same kind of risk assessments is very hard.

Today's AI systems lack any kind of common-sense reasoning, meaning that they don't "understand" the nature of objects and what they do and don't do. The AI has no cognitive capability to realize that people on scooters might veer in front of the car, or that a duck could decide to exit from the nearby pond and waddle into the street. None of these facets are somehow inbred or coded into the AI system.

The vaunted Machine Learning (ML) and Deep Learning (DL) that tends to use Artificial Neural Networks (ANN) is not overcoming per se the lack of common-sense reasoning. These AI capabilities are pattern matchers that try to find recurring patterns in large datasets. If there are enough instances of people riding scooters that veer into traffic, the ML or DL can potentially pick-up on the pattern and therefore be alerted when a scooter is detected in the traffic scene, but suppose the training dataset didn't have those scooter instances, and same goes for the waddling duck.

Of course the other avenue involves programming the AI to put two-plus-two together that if an object is in-motion, such as a scooter, it is worthwhile to figure out the speed, direction, and likelihood that the scooter will intersect with the path of the car. This is a relatively mathematically straightforward operation. Yet it does not include the intention of the scooter rider. You would likely look at the scooter rider and try to guess as to the motives and intentions of the person, doing so to further enhance and embellish your risk assessment.

Devising a mathematically formula for the risk-o-meter is not easy and involves taking into account a myriad of factors, some of which might be important, some of which might be unimportant, and all of which requires juggling hunches and having to on-the-fly determine what's happening and what might happen next.

ASIL And Determining Risk-O-Meter Levels

A well-known standard in the automotive world is the Automotive Safety Integrity Level (ASIL) risk classification scheme, based on an official document referred to as ISO 26262 (there are other related automotive safety standards too, including the forthcoming ISO 21448 or SOTIF).

When determining risk while driving, here's an equation that provides a means to get your arms around risk aspects:

Risk = Severity x (Exposure x Controllability)

Severity is important to consider when ascertaining risk while driving, since you might be heading toward a brick wall that will end-up causing you and your passengers to get smashed and killed (that's a high severity), or the hitting of paint cans on the freeway might be relatively low in severity (it fortunately did not cause any damage under my car and I rolled over them without missing a beat).

Formally, severity is a measure of the potential harm that can arise and can be categorized into: (S0) No injuries, (S1) Light and moderate injuries, (S2) Severe injuries, (S3) Life-threatening and fatal injuries.

Exposure is whether the chances of the incident occurring are substantial versus being unlikely as to you being exposed to the matter (i.e., the state of being in an operational situation of a hazardous nature), such as my rolling over the paint cans was nearly certain as they popped off the truck and into the roadway without any advanced warning, while the alligator that we saw on the road was visible well in-advance and readily avoidable.

Formally, exposure can be divided into: (E0) negligible, (E1) very low, (E2) low, (E3) medium, (E4) high.

Controllability refers to the capability of being able to maneuver the car so as to avoid the pending calamity. This can range from avoiding the situation entirely or be that you can skirt it, or that no matter what you do there is insufficient means to steer, brake, or accelerate and avert the moment.

Formally, controllability can be divided into: (C0) generally controllable, (C1) simply controllable, (C2) normally controllable, (C3) difficult or uncontrollable.

By combining together the three factors of severity, exposure, and controllability, you can arrive at an indication of the risk assessment for a given driving situation. Presumably, we do this in our heads, cognitively, though how we actually do so and whether we even use this kind of logic is debatable since no one really knows how our minds work in this capacity.

Don't be misled into looking at the formula and construing that therefore it is simple to encode this into an AI system. There is a tremendous amount of judgement that goes into how you as a human classify the exposure, the severity, and the controllability.

Conclusion

There is a famous AI ethics discussion point around something called the Trolley Problem. In short, imagine a scenario in which you were able to steer a trolley toward one of two train tracks and at the end of those tracks were people that would get hit by the trolley. If one track led to say five people, while the other track led to only one-person, which way would you steer the trolley?

I mention this philosophical question because autonomous cars are going to confront the same kind of issues when driving on our roadways. There will be situations in which the risks of say hitting a child darting into the street might need to be weighed against the risks of swerving the car to avoid hitting the child but then have the car rollover or ram into a post or wall, injuring or killing the passengers within the driverless car.

What should the AI decide to do?

You can perhaps now discern why the risk-o-meter is a crucial element for the AI system of an autonomous car and also see why it is a difficult capability to concoct.

The next time that you come near to a driverless car, perhaps one that is being tried out on your local public roadways, realize that within the AI system and the coding and the ML or DL, there is something that is undertaking a risk-o-meter like effort and deciding where and what the AI should do about maneuvering the car.

There's no magic involved, it's all software and hardware, and no Wizard of Oz standing behind the curtain.

CHAPTER 3
ERODING CAR DEVOTION
AND
AI SELF-DRIVING CARS

CHAPTER 3

ERODING CAR DEVOTION
AND
AI SELF-DRIVING CARS

There's no secret to the aspect that by-and-large Americans love their cars.

We pamper them in a manner akin to doting after your favored pet dog or cat. We rely upon our beloved cars to get us to work, and to get us to the beach or up into the mountains for hiking, and treasure them for the freedom and independence they can provide.

It's not an easy relationship necessarily.

Sometimes your car plays dead and the engine won't start, or your car hiccups while on the freeway and you end-up sitting in the emergency lane dreading your predicament. Cars are somewhat demanding of attention, requiring that you keep your car in a semblance of shape that it can run on the roadways.

There's definitely a love-hate factor involved, hopefully veering more towards the love side of things, most of the time.

You can go beyond just keeping your car in drivable shape and opt to get outlandish and primp it, if you wish to do so.

Some people drive around in their shined-up and decked out cars, seemingly saying take a look, and do so to either display their pride in their prized possession, or because they want to brag about what they have. Look at me, some cars and their car owners say, such as the Lamborghinis and Mazarakis of this world, and the driver beams at showing off either their wealth or their vaunted status, seeking accolades from those that look upon them and their upscale carriage as they drive among our lowly streets.

Automotive advertising has helped shape our culture to believe that it is manly to drive a certain kind of car. Maybe in the early days of automobile formulation it took a bit of strength or fortitude to drive a car, but you'd be hard pressed to make the case today that you have to be muscular and have strong abs to drive a car, yet somehow the manliness image continues to be promulgated.

For women, car ads have tended to focus on aspects such as bringing together a family via driving a car, and only recently have those ads shifted toward the "manliness" kinds of elements for women such as suggesting that a woman can be free spirited and independent if they own a car or drive a particular brand or model of cars.

Yes, there are lots of old tropes that are gradually shifting or changing as society shifts and changes.

Here's a question for you to consider, namely whether America's love affair with automobiles will be dissolved by the advent of self-driving driverless cars.

This is a debate being argued feverishly in the halls of the automotive realm and for which could dramatically impact how people value cars and even how they perceive themselves.

Let's unpack the debate.

What Might Happen With The Advent Of Driverless Cars

One viewpoint about the advent of driverless autonomous cars, which are ones that driven entirely by the AI automation and there is no human driver involved, suggests that we all will eventually not care about which car we are in.

I'm saying that as a passenger, since you'll no longer be a driver, you won't care about the nature of the car, other than it will get you from point A to point B. You get into an autonomous car, you tell it where you want to go, and the rest of the driving journey you are able to do whatever you wish to do, such as leisurely look out the window or perhaps watch a move being displayed on an interior TV inside the driverless car.

You might own the autonomous car, or you might not.

Some predict that autonomous cars will be used primarily for ridesharing purposes and be owned by large companies that deploy them in fleets. I've argued that I still think individual ownership will occur, wherein you buy an autonomous car to use for your own transportation needs, plus you rideshare it out when you don't need to use it, including while at work or maybe at night while you are sleeping.

If everyone is pretty much using any randomly available autonomous car, presumably it makes having any kind of personal or social bond to cars much less likely. It is akin to no longer owning a pet dog or cat, and instead just borrowing one for a few minutes to tide you over. You aren't probably going to become very emotionally attached to the animal.

So, assuming that we all begin to believe that cars are simply interchangeable mechanical devices for purposes of transportation, out goes the window of any kind of personal pride or attachment to a car. You won't really have anything to brag about.

Also, since you aren't driving anymore, the "manliness" aspects of how you steer or drive a car is eviscerated too.

The AI is essentially taking over the "manliness" if you consider it somehow manly to be able to drive a car. In terms of bringing families together, which as been the predominant feminine ad pitch, well, the kids will be able to get to school on their own via an autonomous car, and a husband can go in an autonomous car to work, and the wife can do likewise, splitting up everyone more so than bringing them together.

For those various reasons, you could make the case that the love affair of cars by Americans is going to become extinct.

Sorry cars, you had a great run, while you were conventional, but once you become sophisticated enough to drive, in an era of AI driverless autonomous cars, no one is going to love you anymore, and instead take you for granted as just a hunk of metal and gears that serves to conveniently tout around people.

Another Side Of The Love Affair Coin Could Emerge

Hold on, some assert, the gloomy forecast of the busted love affair might not be taking into account the full range of factors involved.

Cars will still be providing a sense of freedom and independence.

No matter whether a car is driven by a human or being driven by AI, you can still use the car for mobility purposes. Indeed, some argue that autonomous cars will supercharge our society in terms of mobility, become an economy transformed by increased mobility that has been otherwise suppressed or not viable before, adding the mobility marginalized into the realm of access to mobility.

Can't we then love autonomous cars for their enhanced and expanded mobility, giving us all more freedom than before?

Furthermore, the AI of driverless cars will gradually get better and better at interacting with humans.

Today, we are used to the simplistic and stilted dialogue that you have with an Alexa or a Siri. In the future, driverless cars will presumably carry on interactively with their passengers in a fluid manner, discussing with you where want to go, and likely offering insider tips about local cultural sites to see if you are a tourist, or places to watch out for if you are new to town.

In addition, it is anticipated that the AI systems will personalize to you, the passenger. Each time you get into an autonomous car, the AI will know who you are, along with having your entire record of places you've gone to via driverless cars, and can "converse" with you about how you are doing, how's work coming along, and seemingly know more about you than perhaps you own loved ones (I know this seems creepy, and perhaps it is, but it is akin to what ATM's do today, though of course amplified).

The anthropomorphic aspects might become so powerful that people will not just love their cars, they'll become addicted to their cars.

Here's how. A driverless car can be used presumably 24x7, since there is always a AI driver ready and available to drive you. You can choose to move further away from work and merely have your autonomous car drive you several hours each way, perhaps getting some extra shuteye while in the driverless car. You can work while inside your car, since you aren't driving. Combine these aspects with the AI system human interaction as an added bonding, it could be that you might essentially live inside your driverless car.

That's something that would uproot many of today's discussions about people that are living in their cars.

I would also like to break the assumption that all autonomous cars are going to be of the same shape, size, and exterior look.

There are pundits that say we won't care about the outward appearance of our cars anymore, since we will be riding whichever driverless car happens to be convenient at the time that you need a ride. In their theory, gradually all cars will morph toward being of the same exterior, bland, and the same size and shape, being large enough to accommodate a maximum number of paying ridesharing passengers per driving journey.

Some say that all cars, assuming that we have all driverless cars, will be no more than bubbles within which we will be transported. You'll care about the interiors of the driverless cars, since that's what you'll see and interact with, while the outside of the car will make no difference to you.

I doubt this, though it is a thought-provoking point.

I believe we'll still have car sizes and shapes of all kinds, along with varying exterior looks, and that people will opt to choose which kind of autonomous car they prefer to go in. When you go online to seek an autonomous car for a ride, you'll be able to specify the particulars of what kind of driverless car you want to use.

Admittedly, if you have to wait an additional twenty minutes to get to the grocery store, rather than taking whichever autonomous car happens to be nearer to you, it could be a factor in your selection, but I still think we'll have preferences overall about the look of the car we ride in.

Conclusion

Is the love affair that we have with our cars going to gradually falter and evaporate due to the emergence of driverless autonomous cars?

Yes, some say, since cars will become essentially a commodity that we only care about to the extent that it transports us. You probably don't love your mass transit train that you use to get to work today, so why would you love your ridesharing any-randomly-chosen driverless car that happens to get you to work in the future.

Others say that we'll still love our cars, relishing them for the freedoms they provide, and personalization will no longer be tied to a specific car, but instead become an emotional bond across whole fleets of driverless cars, each one welcoming you and treating you like a king or queen when you get into the autonomous car.

Love affairs can be fickle, and I guess only time will tell whether the beloved conventional car, once tossed onto the heap of ex-loved machines, will be replaced by smooth-talking AI driverless cars.

CHAPTER 4

DRUNK DRIVING RISES WITH SMART CARS

CHAPTER 4

DRUNK DRIVING

RISES WITH SMART CARS

In the United States, approximately 11,000 people will get killed due to drunk driving this year.

That's 30 people, human beings, young and old, male and female, being killed each day of the year.

In terms of the number of people injured due to drunk driving, it's hard to gauge, but some put the number around 750,000 harmed souls each year. Research suggests that Americans are apt to drink and drive quite frequently, doing so on an estimated 121 million such incidents annually.

What can be done about this drunken related driving proneness and calamities?

One of the most oft stated justifications for the advent of driverless autonomous cars is that hopefully the amount of drunk driving related deaths and injuries will drop precipitously.

There are pundits that claim the number should become zero, namely zero injuries and deaths that are drunk driving related, because truly autonomous cars won't have human drivers, thus there's zero chances of drunk driving.

This claim might have validity except for the fact that we aren't going to suddenly have an overnight situation of all driverless autonomous cars and no human driven cars on our roadways. The reality is that with 250 million conventional cars in the hands of Americans today, it will be many years before the emergence of driverless cars will overtake the stock of conventional cars, once autonomous cars start to become practical and available for use.

We need to grapple with the notion that the advent of autonomous cars will be gradual and slowly enter into the mainstream of car traffic.

No one even can say whether it will really be the case that ultimately we'd have only and exclusively driverless cars on our streets. Unless there is an outright ban on conventional cars, the odds are that some subset of the populace will cling to wanting to drive a car themselves and not have the AI be the only driver in-town. Thus, it keeps the door open to drunk driving.

That being said, if the amount of human driving gets smaller and smaller over time (being essentially stepwise replaced by autonomous driving), the volume of possible drunk drivers should be shrinking too.

And, the AI of driverless cars will presumably be shaped-up to deal with suspected drunk drivers that are encountered on the highways and byways. If an AI-run autonomous car spots driving behavior of other nearby traffic that resembles drunk driving, the autonomous car can seek to avoid getting entangled in the potential drunken driving act, along with warning other nearby driverless cars via V2V (vehicle-to-vehicle) electronic communications. This might reduce the odds of the drunk driver injuring or killing others.

In theory, an autonomous car that has detected a potential human driven drunk-driving instance might alert the authorities, generating an urgent electronic communique to 911. Not everyone though is going to be okay with that approach. It would be like having a mobile system that is roaming around aka Big Brother and tattling on other cars.

Yes, the AI might be right in terms of gauging and reporting on a drunk driver, but it could also be wrong and falsely accusing a human driver of something they are innocent of.

So far in this discussion I've been focusing on driverless autonomous cars.

For truly driverless cars, ones that are considered at the Level 4 and Level 5 of automated driving, there isn't a human driver and the AI is doing all of the driving. That's a pretty clear-cut circumstance of ensuring that there is not a human driver at the wheel that might be DUI and veering towards disaster.

Meanwhile, on our roads today, the conventional cars of a Level 2 capability are starting to be outdated by the recent introduction of more automated ADAS (Advanced Driver Assistance Systems) in Level 3 cars.

I have unfortunate news to report that the soon to emerge Level 3 semi-autonomous cars are not only likely to allow drunk driving to continue, there's a solid possibility it could exacerbate drunken driving and make it even more prevalent.

Let me explain why.

Seemingly A Paradox Of Level 3 And Drunk Driving

I'm sure you might be puzzled that somehow drunk driving might actually worsen when there is increased automaton in our cars as Level 3 semi-autonomous vehicles gain popularity.

Shouldn't better automation mean that we'll have less injuries and deaths due to drunken driving?

It stands to reason that theoretically it should.

I'll give you a rather poignant example of why I assert that drunk driving might worsen with Level 3 cars.

A reporter was recently interviewing the CEO of General Motors (GM), Mary Barra, doing so while the two of them were in one of GM's semi-autonomous cars on a closed track or proving ground. The reporter tried out some of the driving features that included letting the automation drive the car, even though the reporter was still considered the true driver of the car and retained responsibility for the driving act per se.

At one point, the reporter turned to Mary and asked if the automation was essentially a designated driver that could take over the driving in case the human driver was drunk.

I'd bet that a lot of people harbor such a belief.

Indeed, overall, I've predicted that the Level 3 semi-autonomous cars are going to lull human drivers into falsely believing that the automation is capable in ways that it most certainly is not capable. Humans are humans, and if they start to rely upon the automation, you can be assured that they will fall further and further into the mental trap that the car can drive itself, even though at Level 3 it cannot do so.

Essentially, the Level 3 has all of the trappings that seem like it can drive the car.

Now, I realize that some of you are saying that people will figure out the boundaries of what their Level 3 car can and cannot do. People are smart, they can get the drift of things. They will reason about their Level 3 cars and not allow complacency to overcome their judgment.

Besides my perhaps pessimistic view that I don't quite have the same faith in humanity as the aforementioned notion, let's also add something else into the equation.

Let's add being drunk.

Even if I grant you that a completely sober person will be a good driver in a Level 3 car, and won't get themselves mired into letting their attention drift away from the driving task, which I still say is a big if, but anyway suppose the person is intoxicated.

Do you really believe that an intoxicated person won't be likely to assume that their Level 3 car can become their designated driver?

How This Phenomena Increases Drunk Driving

My assertion is that people will not only make mental mistakes of assuming their Level 3 car can handle the driving for them in everyday situations when the human driver is sober, it will also and especially happen when those human drivers are drunk.

Someone is at their local bar and celebrating a promotion that they had gotten at work that day. Alcohol is flowing.

After becoming tipsy, the celebrant wanders out to their Level 3 car in the parking lot.

With a conventional car, the person might have second thoughts about getting behind the wheel. In this case, given the staying-in-lane capabilities of the automation, the lane changing features, and so on, the driver "decides" that whatever impairment they have will undoubtedly be handled by the Level 3 ADAS aspects.

It would be an easy mental judgement to make, particularly when you are sloshed.

Overall, the Level 3 will create a false impression for those in a drunken state of mind that the automation will be their fellow designated driver, making up for whatever the drunken driver might have difficulties handling.

I realize that some of you might be suggesting that in some respects this is actually a partially valid notion. Indeed, there is a chance that the automation will be able warn the drunken driver that they are weaving out of their lane. That's good.

The hard thing to macroscopically calculate will be how much might the Level 3 automation be able to aid in keeping a drunk driver from getting into a drunken disaster versus how much will the Level 3 entice drunk drivers to try driving their car when they shouldn't be on the road at all.

For every instance of the Level 3 serving as an on-board safety cushion to indirectly detect and warn when a driver is driving erratically, how many instances will we have of drunken drivers that purposely drove because they assumed the Level 3 would act as a driver that would save them from their own drunkenness?

I'd tend to wager that the Level 3 won't be sufficient to end-up overall preventing drunk driving injuries and deaths, in spite of its warning capabilities and in some cases its ability to undertake simplistic driving chores.

I'd double-down on that wager and assert that the Level 3 will be so alluring that it will encourage people that would not have considered doing drunk driving and now make them susceptible to doing so.

In short, you've got people that would drink and drive not matter whether they have a conventional car or a Level 3, and they'll still be getting sadly onto our roads. The Level 3 won't be sufficient to overcome their drunken driving antics and they'll still on-the-whole commit drunk driving incidents.

Plus, you'll now have an added contingent of the populace that normally would have been more circumspect about driving while drunk, and they will falsely get behind the wheel of a car under the mistaken and drunken mindset that their Level 3 car will save them.

As a result, the volume of drunk driving will rise, commitment with a rise in injuries and deaths due to drunk driving.

Conclusion

While on the path toward true autonomous cars, we are going to have semi-autonomous cars that are neither here nor there in terms of the muddying of what is automated versus what is not automated for the driving task.

In the gray area of Level 3, people are going to assume that the Level 3 can act as a co-sharing buddy that will keep the human driver from getting into driving trouble.

Drivers might be tempted more so to drive when they should not be driving.

After all these years of trying to drum away at don't drink and drive, there will be a segment of society that believes this mantra is no longer applicable because they happen to have a Level 3 car.

Will we need to put breath analyzers on all Level 3 cars to try and ensure that people don't let themselves become wayward and aim toward driving when they should not be driving?

If the use of breath analyzers seems over-the-top to you, I suppose the Level 3 cars could try to use some other means to ferret out a drunk driver sitting in the driver's seat.

With facial recognition and a camera pointed at the head of the driver, the automation might be able to detect facial expressions indicative of being intoxicated.

Furthermore, the Level 3 could also potentially use voice systems such as the Alexa and Siri kinds of Natural Language Processing (NLP) systems that are becoming ubiquitous.

Via the NLP, the Level 3 car could ask questions of the driver, and by analyzing their voice patterns and what they say, it is conceivable that the automation could ascertain the chances of the driver being drunk.

Will though people be accepting of having their own cars trying to challenge them as to whether they are sober enough to drive?

It seems hard to believe that people en masse will agree to such technology.

Maybe the tech would be offered on Level 3 cars and people could choose to switch it on or off.

Of course, you could argue that those that would be prone to drink and drive are probably the ones that would permanently switch off those features.

Thus, it would only be those that wouldn't drive drunk that would end-up having them switched on, pretty much defeating the purpose of those "early detection" systems for preventing drunk drivers from driving ahead.

Perhaps people will change their ways and with the advent of Level 3 we'll see that drunk driving reduces, though I'm not holding my breath about this possibility.

I would suggest that you'd need to be rather optimistic about human behavior, the very same human behavior that already is killing 11,000 people per year in the United States and injuring another several hundreds of thousands of people.

CHAPTER 5
DRIVER'S DIFFICULTIES AND SMART CARS

CHAPTER 5

DRIVER'S DIFFICULTIES AND SMART CARS

We've all grown-up with the understanding that when you move the steering wheel of a car it will cause the car to turn this way or that way, as based on how you opted to steer. Likewise, we take at face value that when you push down on the gas pedal it will make the car accelerate. Equally assumed is the notion that if you jam your foot onto the brakes, the car will seek to stop.

This is Driving 101, for which even novice teenage drivers are able to quickly grasp how to access and use the everyday standard driving controls of a conventional car.

There are approximately 225 million licensed drivers in the United States alone, and all of them have come to accept and assume that the driving controls are essentially the same on every car they happen to drive. I'd bet that the car you own works in the same simple manner, and a friend's car likely does too, and if you rent a car there is almost no "learning curve" about driving the rented vehicle.

Humans are able to interchangeably operate just about any conventional car, doing so without having to read an owner's manual or get a 15-minute on-the-spot training course.

Sure, you might need a few moments to adjust the mirrors and figure out how to play music on the car radio. You might fumble to discover the seat adjustment knobs or have a difficult time initially with the windshield wipers or how to open the trunk. None of those facets are particularly germane to the driving task and presumably you can merely hop into the driver's seat, start the engine, and drive off the lot of a rental car agency in no time flat.

The latest and emerging souped-up driving controls for cars are changing that unspoken, always assumed, and long tested and proven belief that the controls are the controls.

With the advent of Level 3 semi-autonomous cars, known for having Advanced Driving Assistance Systems (ADAS), you can toss out the window what you thought you knew about driving a car, at least with respect to what you and the automation are co-sharing.

Whereas to-date the ADAS pretty much left you in the driver's seat, and was quietly assisting in a manner that was generally subtle and rare, now it is going to be sitting right next you, taking on more of the driving task and messing with your mind.

Consider Your Theory Of Mind About The Car

Whether you realize it or not, you have in your mind a so-called "Theory of Mind" about your car.

Theory of Mind is a phrase commonly used to refer to the aspect of how you perceive that other people or things work in terms of what is in their minds. When I play rock-paper-scissors with my kids, I tend to know what is in their minds as to what they will show or roll next, having played the game with them seemingly endlessly. Over time, I figure out what they maybe are thinking, such as if they've done three scissors in a row, they are bound to use next a rock.

Though your car doesn't have a mind per se, it does do various mechanical and electronic operations that give it a kind of behavior for which you could stretch the word "mind" and say that the car is being somewhat mindful.

I am decidedly not saying the car is intelligent or exhibits anything equating to human intelligence. The car is operating with extremely limited behaviors and yet it is important that you, the human driver, be familiar with what the car will do and when it will take its own actions.

One of my favorite examples involves ABS (Anti-Lock Brake System) that most contemporary cars now have included as standard on the vehicle. The ABS is supposed to come to your rescue as a driver and aid in slowing or stopping the car when you need to brake rapidly.

Most people are accustomed to pumping their brakes when they get onto an icy road if they are losing traction with the roadway surface, but that's not the recommended approach when you have ABS. The ABS has speed sensors that are mounted onto the wheels and will automatically pulse the brakes for you when it detects skidding activity and so you are able to merely push persistently on the brake pedal and have no need to do a pumping action yourself.

Here's some key illuminated points using the ABS as an example about Theory of Mind:

Human drivers tend to not understand how the ABS works and thus are often clueless about what to do or not do as it relates to their ABS capability in the car.

Even for those human drivers that might comprehend the nature of ABS, once they find themselves in a high-pressure situation their reactive emotion can overpower whatever logical understanding they have, and they tend to react unthinkingly.

Legally, cars built after the year 2013 are supposed to have ABS, as mandated by the National Highway Traffic Safety Administration (NHTSA), and so you presumably would know right away whether the car you are driving has ABS or not, but this also assumes that you've been astute enough to discover the year of the car's making and then put two-plus-two together to realize there is or is not ABS (depending upon the year of the car).

Okay, so we have a situation involving quite rudimentary automation, the ABS, and for which human drivers often don't know what it does, aren't sure of when it will come to play, don't understand how they should react to it reacting, and might anyway in a panic ignore or forget about the ABS, along with not being sure if the ABS feature is actually on the car they are driving.

It seems obvious that this could be a problem, given that the human driver is supposed to be responsible for the ship, or the car, and yet the captain that's running things doesn't fully realize what a feature does and nor how it and they as a driver are co-sharing a vital piece of the driving task.

Fortunately, in the case of ABS, we can all get along without knowing the ABS and just continue driving our cars due to the rather subtle and infrequent need to invoke the ABS. Thus, though there is a sizable Theory of Mind gap, in day-to-day driving the gap doesn't emerge as a disorder and doesn't impact the usual driving activities.

That's not going to be the case with the ADAS that's emerging with Level 3 semi-autonomous cars.

Advanced Automation And Your Blind Spot

With the emergence of more sophisticated automation and ADAS, a Level 3 semi-autonomous car is gradually going to be chockful with lots of potentially handy driving assistants, as though you have a bunch of added hands to aid in driving a car.

There is no single standard that states exactly what an ADAS package consists of, and so you need to somehow become aware of what a car with ADAS has on it.

You might have a collision warning system that lets you know if you are about to hit another car. You might have a lane departure warning system that beeps at you when you wander out of your lane. You might have a wrong-way driving warning system. And so on.

Not only do you need to go out of your way to know what's available on the car that you happen to be driving, you also need to understand a Theory of Mind about what each of those ADAS features does, and what you need to do about what each of those features.

To-date, most of these ADAS features are warnings that try to alert you, the driver, about some untoward situation that is brewing. It is then up to you to decide whether the warning is bona fide, and you also need to determine what driving action to take due to being forewarned by the warning system.

We are now entering into a time when the ADAS feature will begin to make decisions on your behalf and will then proactively takeover the driving task to help you out.

In a manner of speaking, you could say that the ABS was similar to this notion, since the ABS typically pulses the brakes on your behalf, which maybe you know is happening or not, but anyway it is taking an overt driving action, regardless of your awareness about the matter. This is usually fine and you blissfully are simply happy that something good seems to happen, as magically performed by the ABS.

Will this be true though as the ADAS becomes more at the forefront of the driving task?

Let's explore the role of the emerging ADAS features for blind spot aspects.

We've all had moments of failing to see a car or a bicyclist in our blind spots and nearly run into those innocent souls. In spite of our overall realization that we should always be checking our blind spots when making a driving maneuver, it is commonplace to forget to do so. Or, maybe you checked the blind spot a split second ago, and by the time you perform a lane changing maneuver, the once clear blind spot is now occupied, but you might not realize it since you are still under the (false) impression that your blind spot is empty.

Here's a question for you, which I'll make as multiple choice.

For the state-of-the-art ADAS blind spot feature, what does it do:

- Alerts if there is something in the blind spot when you are about to maneuver

- Begins with a mild alert like a soft tone and then escalates to flashing at you and loud beeping

- Will apply added force to the steering wheel to make it harder for you to continue your maneuver

- Will prevent the underway maneuver by steering as needed regardless of your steering

The answer is that it could be any of those choices.

Yes, the choices include not merely a warning action such as tones, beeps, or flashing indicators, but also now are beginning to include more direct driving actions by the automation.

This includes making the steering wheel harder to turn, which hopefully then gets the human driver to realize somethings is afoot and will not therefore continue to steer toward the objects in the blind spot.

The more intrusive action is if the blind spot ADAS feature decides to not merely warn you, and instead does a real-time takeover of the driving action itself. In this case, the blind spot detector becomes an actual co-driver of the car. Pretend that you had another person in the car that was also at the driving controls. You and that other person are co-driving or co-sharing the driving task, except in this case it is a bare bones piece of automation.

Recall my earlier points about the Theory of Mind and ABS, let's recast those points in a larger scope manner:

Human drivers tend to not understand how the advanced ADAS features work and thus are often clueless about what to do or not do as it relates to the advanced ADAS capability in a car.

Even for those human drivers that might comprehend the nature of their advanced ADAS features, once they find themselves in a high-pressure situation their reactive emotion can overpower whatever logical understanding they have, and they tend to react unthinkingly.

You have no particular way to immediately know what advanced ADAS features are included into a car, you have no immediate way to realize what those features will do, and those features can vary from one brand of car to the next, and even differ on any given car if the features are able to be turned on-or-off (plus, many allow parameter settings as to sensitivity levels, etc.)

Conclusion

The world is changing, especially the driving world.

You cannot continue to assume that the steering steers as you've always experienced it, and nor that the brakes and the accelerator will respond as they have in the past. You'll now have an on-board co-driver of sorts, advanced ADAS, for which you'll need to come up-to-speed about the idiosyncratic aspects of those features.

Presumably, when you buy a car, you'll have to spend the needed time to learn about the advanced ADAS, though we'll have to wait and see whether people will really do so, whereas they might just "wing it" and try out the features as they begin driving the car around town.

The same notion applies to renting a car, namely that maybe the rental agency will offer to show you the advanced ADAS, but you might be rushed and won't spend the time to learn it, or you might assume that all ADAS are the same and thus skip the added training.

We also don't yet really know how people will deal with the proactive ADAS driving aspects and whether they might fight with the automation in moments of dire straits.

If you don't have a proper Theory of Mind about why the car is trying to turn you away from your desired driving action, you might not acquiesce and instead fight to make the turn as you see fit.

If you ever wondered why some of the automakers and tech firms are focusing more so on Level 4 and Level 5, which involves fully autonomous cars that have no human driving and no co-shared driving involved, you now know why.

Some believe that there should be just one driver of a car, either a human driver as unaided by a co-driving piece of automation, or an AI-run driving system.

When you try to put two drivers into the same driving seat, it is bound to create troubles.

Those troubles are exacerbated when the human driver has an inadequate Theory of Mind about their co-driving automation buddy.

The mental muscle memory that humans have about driving conventional cars is going to make for predicaments when they deal with the variability of advanced ADAS.

Like the old story about the frog that doesn't realize it is inside a boiling pot of water that is gradually being brought to a burning boil, human drivers are potentially heading down that same path with the gradual introduction of advances in ADAS.

We need to all be aware that the pot is boiling and we're all in it together.

.

CHAPTER 6

MILLENNIALS AREN'T AS CAR CRAZED AS BABY BOOMERS

CHAPTER 6

MILLENNIALS AREN'T
AS CAR CRAZED
AS BABY BOOMERS

The automotive industry is not very happy with Millennials and Gen Z.

It seems that in comparison to the Baby Boomers and Gen X, the latest up-and-coming generations are less car crazed and thus creating great difficulties and consternation for those that are making automobiles.

Purchases of cars by the younger set are dropping precipitously. Survey after survey shows that the latest generations don't put car ownership particularly high on their list of things to do.

Perhaps worse too is that those potential drivers aren't even pursuing getting driver's licenses as earnestly as prior generations, meaning that the pipeline of drivers that would want to buy a car is not flowing in the same guaranteed manner as in the past.

Chatting with Millennials and Gen Z often reveals that they actually eschew driving. If they can avoid having to drive a car, they will happily and eagerly find a means around doing so.

You can contrast this viewpoint to those of us from the prior generations.

We grew-up believing that having and owning a car was a crucial part of life, something that was a must-do. Getting a driver's license was a rite-of-passage, showcasing that you were progressing from being a kid to becoming an adult.

Sitting behind the steering wheel was a source of pride. You were in-charge of a multi-ton beast, demonstrating your strength and virility (for both men and woman!). The car gave you street cred among your late-teens peers. It was also a source of freedom, being able to escape from the overshadowing heavy-handed control of your parents and stood as a path to your rightful independence.

You can toss out most of those now classic but outdated tropes.

There has been a sea-shift emerging about the cultural norms and attitudes toward cars and the act of driving.

No sense in complaining about it, and instead might as well get prepared. As they say, it is the new norm.

Let's unpack why this is happening and also consider what impact the advent of self-driving driverless cars might have on this overarching trend.

The Mindset Change About Cars

I am often asked whether there is one specific reason that the latest generations are not avidly courting cars and driving.

I'd say that it is an intertwined set of whys and wherefores, which at a macro-level perspective you could potentially suggest is "the reason," but I don't buy into the notion that there is really a single thread that is the sole instigator for what is happening.

I'll rattle off the myriad of overlapping aspects, all of which are juicing each other and causing an upheaval of sorts:

- **Less enamored of making large capital purchases.** The latest gens are often saddled with student debt and aren't interested in digging into the debt abyss any further. Even if they have the dough, they saw what happened in the most recent recession and are skittish about letting their savings go toward a thing called a car (they know that the asset will drop in value the moment they drive it off-the-lot).

- **Ridesharing provides a viable alternative.** The seemingly ubiquitous availability of ridesharing, which perhaps is more appropriately coined as ride-hailing (since there's not that much sharing of rides taking place per se), makes life easy for you if you don't perchance own a car. Your mobile app brings a car right to your doorstep.

- **Don't want worries about car glitches and burdens.** Think about the headaches that owning a car can cause. Where do you park your car and how much will that cost you? You need to get car insurance, yuk. You need to figure out what to do if the car goes awry, and deal with the bewildering morass of auto repair options. A car equates to one enormous bag of hassles, and so it makes sense to elude it.

- **Driving is not fun, it's a chore.** Perhaps one of the biggest differences seems to be that the recent generations perceive driving as a chore, something you do to get from point A to point B. Prior generations were led to believe that driving was fun and a form of artistic expression. The latest drivers are more down-to-earth and see driving as perfunctory.

- **FOMO strikes the car equation.** Fear Of Missing Out (FOMO) has taken root in the latest generations. This translates into meaning that whatever you are doing now, it might be the wrong thing to do, since you are missing out on something better that you ought to be doing. Consider how FOMO applies to buying a car. You might buy a car that at the moment was the most exciting model and choice, and yet two months later something cooler comes along. Darn it, you missed out, and thus it is better to not get "stuck" making a choice at all.

- **Getting a car is ugly and brutal.** Everyone knows via movies and TV that walking onto a car dealership lot is akin to entering into a den of snakes and scary horrors (that's the enduring image being repeatedly conveyed, true or not as to what actually transpires). You'll get taken advantage of. You'll be overwhelmed with arcane paperwork. This is why there are now emerging online means to buy a car and try to make the process less arduous and frightening, including even having the car delivered to you, rather than having to go to it.

- **Car is a mystery of mechanical mechanisms.** It seems that the prior generations are passing along less and less about how to go under-the-hood of a car, eventually leading to the latest generations not knowing how a car works. In fact, the latest gen doesn't care how it works, and mainly focuses on the output it can produce. This means that you become distant from any emotional or personal attachment to a car, since there's no sense of workmanship that you changed the oil or put on a spare tire. Those tasks are done by someone else for you, thankfully, and it just magically is undertaken by them.

- **Don't like the hard sell.** In the past, automobiles were often marketed and sold with the same selling fervor reserved for selling swamp land. The latest gen knows about this. The latest gen is a cynical bunch that doesn't believe wild claims, or at least gets turned-off when they smell it happening. Pundits have said that the latest gen prefers authenticity. You've likely noticed that the car ads are playing that angle now and been less over-the-top about their vehicles than they used to be (well, some of the time).

- **Traffic is terrible and so driving is exasperating.** There was a day once that you could drive your car with the windows rolled down and enjoy the wind and push the pedal to the metal. More cars came along. Roads haven't changed much. Today's driver is going to find themselves in traffic, stuck in snarls and moving at a snail's pace. Being a driver is worse than doing a chore, it is like having your teeth pulled. The latest gen figures outsource the driving to those that are willing to endure it.

- **Ecological and ecosystem awareness.** The latest gen is aware that gasoline powered cars are emitting harmful emissions, and though they also know that it is much improved in comparison to prior years, nonetheless it is still a bad thing. They are interested in EV's as an ecological matter, but also unsure about EV's since it hasn't spread fully and presents other difficulties like charging the EV and what do on longer drives. So, they decidedly don't want to get a polluting car, and nor are they willing to commit just yet to the EV's.

- **No bragging rights, maybe stigma instead.** There was a time that you could brag that you got a driver's license and could drive a car. You would brag that you drove your car to the mountains, or to the desert, or to the beach, or on vacation, and so on. Everybody has a driver's license now. Everybody can drive to those places if they want to do so. There isn't any bragging now, and in fact it could be a kind of stigma, such as why did you drive that distance when you've got this-or-that here, what a waste.

- And there's more. I could list additional points, but it hopefully is apparent that shifting aspects of our society and culture have changed the dynamics about owning a car and driving a car.

Okay, I've provided you with a taste of the underlying elements that are driving the latest generations away from driving, plus why they are shunning owning a car.

For those of you that might say that you know a latest gen and the person doesn't fit to all of those causes and concerns, well, yes, I wasn't suggesting that every person fits to every one of those points. Generally, I'm saying that those points are significant contributors and in their respective parts and pieces pretty much fits to the latest gen on a predominant basis (individual exceptions allowed).

What Happens With The Advent Of Driverless Cars

The aforementioned points are contextually dealing with conventional cars and everyday commonplace driving.

The million-dollar question is how things will change once we have self-driving driverless cars.

I'm referring to autonomous cars that are driven by an AI system and there is no human driver needed. Indeed, some argue that human drivers won't be able to drive a car, even if they want to do so, since cars will no longer have any human accessible driving controls (this is debatable).

If you are wondering whether the latest gen is maybe holding out until driverless cars appear, which thusly would be another explanation for their hesitancy of buying a car today, along with why they don't seem to care as much about being able to drive, I'd say that it is somewhat farfetched to make such a claim, today.

I don't think it is much of a factor right now, but I would fervently argue that once true self-driving cars begin to appear and have some prevalence, you can certainly expect the latest gen will likely take into account that the "movement" has begun.

Would you go out and buy a conventional car or even a semi-autonomous car, if you knew for sure that fully autonomous cars were now ready and able to be obtained?

Don't think you would.

Also, if driverless cars were seen as becoming available fast enough, would you go to the trouble to get a driver's license, unless or only as a form of federally approved form of ID?

Probably you'd get it just for the ID purposes.

This then takes us to another controversial topic, namely whether the latest gen will no longer buy a car at all, and instead rely completely on ride-hailing or ridesharing via the use of autonomous cars.

Many pundits are predicting that individual ownership of cars is going to disappear like an extinct dinosaur. The view is that driverless cars will be owned by large companies, either the automakers themselves or ridesharing firms or today's car rental firms (transformed) or other conglomerates will get into the game.

These owners will have fleets of driverless cars. They will position their autonomous cars in places to make as much money as possible, doing so one ride at a time. It could get ugly, though, since you might have clogs of driverless cars, all vying to get your ridership, flowing inside cities and neighborhoods, trolling and roaming to find the next paying passenger.

My view is somewhat contrarian about the ownership question.

I've stated that it seems to me that there is a grand opportunity for individuals to own a car in a manner that they had not done previously. Right now, you own a car and it sits around 95% of the time doing nothing, other than waiting for you to use it. That's quite a costly asset to own.

In the future, you buy a driverless car and when you are at work or sleeping at home during the evening, you put it onto a ridesharing or ride-hailing network. It goes off to make you money when you don't need it, and you bring it back to you when you want it to drive you around (this could include barter trading with other such driverless car owners).

I anticipate a large cottage industry of individual owners that are hopeful of augmenting their existing pay by using their driveress car.

This also explains the usual retort that I get on this topic that the average person won't be able to afford a driverless car, which even though no one yet knows what they will cost, whatever the cost might be will now become an investment. Buying a car today is not really an investment, most of the time, while a driverless car is a type of asset that you can purchase and anticipate will bring in revenue. Imagine that the type of loan you would get is different than today, since it's not just the car, it's also the revenue stream that the car will presumably derive.

Conclusion

I believe that the genie is out of the bottle in terms of getting the latest generations to somehow turn back the clock and embrace the joys of driving.

Plus, once true driverless cars emerge, they aren't going to be driving anyway (presumably).

The latest gen is going to continue to find ways to avoid driving when they can afford to do so. They will likewise tend to avoid owning a car.

That being said, if my prediction about the revenue potential from owning a driverless car makes sense, you can bet that the latest gen is not going to sit on the sidelines while others are making money off of getting a driverless car.

If nothing else, FOMO will move them in the direction of seeking to own a car, though primarily for its cash generating advantages.

What I hope to not see is trickery about getting those desperate to find a second income into signing up for faux driverless cars on a vacuous promise of it, akin to perhaps buying a timeshare that someone shows pretty brochures and yet the condos aren't built, the land isn't bought up, and the matter is more of a dream than it is yet a reality.

CHAPTER 7

RISKS OF

AI SELF-DRIVING CARS

CHAPTER 7

RISKS OF

AI SELF-DRIVING CARS

I've had readers contact me asking about the level of risk associated with today's self-driving cars.

In prior columns, my indication was that the risk level is high at this juncture and that you should be cautious and mindful of the risks involved.

Let's clarify right away that there are not as yet any true self-driving driverless cars, none certainly at the Level 5 stature, and so when I refer to your going for a ride in a self-driving car of today it would be one that might barely be considered at a Level 4.

The Level 4 is a constrained or limited variant of what you might imagine a true autonomous car to consist of, and allows for the automaker or tech firm to stipulate that the driverless capabilities will only be viable in particular circumstances (those circumstances are more formerly known as ODD's or Operational Design Domains).

For public roadway tryouts, most of the Level 4 driverless cars include a human back-up driver. The purpose of the human back-up driver is to closely monitor the actions of the self-driving car and intervene as needed to aid in promoting safety during a driving journey.

As such, if you went for a ride in a self-driving car of today, you normally would be accompanied by a human back-up driver, someone presumably trained and alert that is ready to takeover the driving from the AI system. This admittedly takes some of the "excitement" out of the riding experience in that you aren't reliant entirely on the AI system to do the driving, but at the same time this is a useful precautionary move to protect you, plus in many states it is a requirement by-and-large for public roadway tryouts (there are exceptions).

To go for a ride in a self-driving car and do so without a human back-up driver, you would likely need to arrange for a ride at a closed track or proving ground. The companies making the AI systems of self-driving cars are at times practicing and experimenting with their autonomous car systems via the use of a special track that allows for a controlled environment.

Risk Is Everywhere

When referring to risk, it is important to realize that we experience risk throughout our daily lives.

Some people joke that they won't leave their house because it is too risky to go outside, but this offhanded remark overlooks the truth that there is risk while sitting comfortably inside your home. At any moment, an earthquake could shake your house into the dust. While sitting in your living room, an airplane flying overhead could falter and crash into your domicile.

I don't want to seem like a doom-and-gloom person, but my point hopefully is well-taken, namely that the chances of an adverse or unwelcome loss or injury is always at our fingertips and ready to occur.

You absorb risk by being alive and breathing air. Risk is all around you and you are enveloped in it. Those that think they only incur risk when they say go for a walk or otherwise undertake action are sadly mistaken.

No matter what you are doing, sleeping or awake, inside or outside of a building, even if locked away in a steel vault and trying to hide from risk, it is still there, on your shoulder, and at any moment you could suddenly suffer a heart attack or the steel vault might fall and you'd get hurt as an occupant inside it.

This brings us to the equally important point that there is absolute risk and there is relative risk.

We often fall into the mental trap of talking about absolute risk and scare ourselves silly. It is better to discuss relative risk, providing a sense of balance or tradeoff about the risks involved in a matter.

For example, I had earlier stated that I believe the risk of your going for a ride in today's self-driving cars is high, yet you can't know for sure what I mean by the notion of "high" related to the risk involved.

Is the risk associated with being inside a self-driving car considered less or more than say going in an airplane or taking a ride on a boat? By describing the risk in terms of its relative magnitude or amount as it relates to other activities or matters, you can get a more realistic gauge of the risk that someone else is alluding to.

I'd like to then bring up these three measures for this discussion about risk:

R1: Risk associated with a human driving a conventional car

R2: Risk associated with AI driving a self-driving autonomous car

R3: Risk associated with a human & AI co-sharing driving of a car

Let's unpack those risk aspects.

Relative Risk Associated With Self-Driving Cars

We can use R1 as a baseline, since it is the risk associated with a human driving a conventional car.

Whenever you go for a drive in your conventional car, you are incurring the risk associated with you making a mistake and crashing into someone else, or, despite your best driving efforts, there might be someone that crashes into you. Likewise, when you get into someone else's car, such as ridesharing via Uber or Lyft, you are absorbing the risk that the ridesharing driver is going to get into a car accident of one kind or another.

Consider the R2, which is the risk associated with a true self-driving autonomous car.

Most everyone involved in self-driving cars and that cares about the advent of driverless cars are hoping that autonomous cars are going to be safer than human driven cars, meaning that there will presumably less deaths and injuries due to cars, less car crashes, etc.

You could assert that the risk associated with self-driving cars is hoped to be less than the risk associated with human driven conventional cars.

I'll express this via the notation of: R2 < R1

This is aspirational and indicates that we are all hoping that the risk R2 is going to be less than the risk R1.

Indeed, some would argue that it should be this: R2 << R1

This means that the R2 risk, involving the AI driving of a driverless car, would be a lot less, substantially less than the risk of a human driving a conventional car, R1.

You've perhaps heard some pundits that have said this: R2 = 0

Those pundits are claiming that there will be zero fatalities and zero injuries once we have true driverless self-driving cars.

I've debunked this myth in many of my speeches and writings. There is not any reasonable way to get to zero. If a self-driving car comes upon a situation whereby a pedestrian unexpectedly leaps in front of the driverless car while in-motion, the physics bely being able to stop or avoid hitting the person and so there will be at least a non-zero chance of fatalities and injuries.

In short, here's what I'm suggesting so far in this discussion:

- R2 = 0 is false and misleading, it won't happen

- R2 < R1 is aspirational for the near-term

- R2 << R1 is aspirational for the long term

Some believe that we will ultimately have only true self-driving cars on our roadways, and we will somehow ban conventional cars, leading to a Utopian world of exclusively autonomous cars. Maybe, but I wouldn't hold your breath about that.

The world is going to consist of conventional cars and true self-driving cars, for the foreseeable future, and thus we will have human driven cars in the midst of AI-driven cars, or you could say we'll have AI-driven cars in the midst of human driven cars.

Bringing In The Risk Of Co-Sharing Driving

There's an added twist that needs to be included, namely the advent of Level 3 cars, consisting of Advanced Driver-Assistance Systems (ADAS), which provide AI-like capabilities that are utilized in a co-sharing arrangement with a human driver. The ADAS augments the capabilities of a human driver.

To clarify, the Level 3 requires that a licensed-to-drive human driver must be present in the driver's seat of the car. Plus, the human driver is considered the responsible party for the driving task. You could say that the AI system and the human driver are co-sharing the driving effort.

Keep in mind that this does not allow for the human driver to fall asleep or watch videos while driving, since the human driver is always expected to be alert and active as the co-sharing driver.

I have forewarned that Level 3 is going to be troublesome for us all. You can fully anticipate that many human drivers will be lulled into relying upon the ADAS and will therefore let their own guard down while driving. The ADAS will suddenly try to get the human driver to take over the driving controls, which the human driver will now be mentally adrift of the driving situation, and the human driver will not take appropriate evasive action in-time.

In any case, I'm going to use R3 to reflect the risk of the human and AI co-sharing the driving task.

Most everyone is hoping that the co-sharing arrangement is going to make human drivers be safer, presumably because the ADAS is going to provide a handy "buddy driver" and overcome many of today's human solo driving issues.

Here's what people assume:

- $R3 < R1$

- $R3 << R1$

In other words, the co-sharing effort will be less risky than a conventional car with a solo human driver, and maybe even be a lot less risky.

Down-the-road, the thinking is that true driverless cars, ones that are driven solely by the AI system, will be less risky than not only conventional cars being driven by humans, but even less risky than the Level 3 cars that involve a co-sharing of the driving task.

Thus, people hope this will become true:

- R2 < R3

- R2 << R3

Overall, this is the aim when you consider all three types of driving aspects:

R2 < R3 < R1

R2 << R3 << R1

Thus, this is an assertion that ultimately AI driven autonomous cars (R2) are going to be less risky than co-shared driven cars (R3) and for which is less risky than conventional human-driven cars (R1), aiming to be a lot less risky throughout.

Here then is the full annotated list of these equation-like aspects:

$R2 = 0$ -- a false claim that AI autonomous cars won't have any crashes

$R2 < R1$ -- aspirational near-term, AI driven cars less risky than human driven cars

$R2 << R1$ -- aspirational long-term, AI driven cars a lot less risky than human driven cars

$R3 < R1$ – aspirational near-term, co-shared driven cars less risky than human-solo

$R3 << R1$ – aspirational long-term, co-shared driven cars lot less risky than human-solo

$R2 < R3$ – aspirational near-term, AI driven cars less risky than co-shared driven cars

$R2 << R3$ – aspirational long-term, AI driven cars lot less risky than co-shared driven cars

$R2 < R3 < R1$ – aspirational near-term, AI car less risky than co-shared less risky than human-solo

$R2 << R3 << R1$ – aspirational long-term, AI car lot less risky than co-shared and human-solo

Today's Risk Aspects Of Self-Driving Cars

My equations are indicated as the aspirational goals of automating the driving of cars.

We aren't there yet.

When you go for a ride in a self-driving car that has a human back-up driver, you are somewhat embracing the R3 risk category, but not quite.

The human back-up driver is not per se acting as though they are in a Level 3 car, one in which they would be actively co-sharing the driving task, and instead are serving as a "last resort" driver in case the AI of the self-driving car seems to need a "disengagement" (industry parlance for a human driver that takes over from the AI during a driving journey).

It is an odd and murky position.

You aren't directly driving the car. You are observing and waiting for a moment wherein either the AI suddenly hands you the ball, or you of your own volition suspect or believe that it is vital to takeover for the AI.

Some might say that I should add a fourth category to my list, an R4, which would be akin to the R3, though it is a co-sharing involving the human driver being more distant of the driving task.

Another approach would be to delineate differing flavors of the R3.

For example, some automakers and tech firms are putting into place a monitoring capability that tries to track the attentiveness of the human driver that is supposed to be co-sharing the driving task. This might involve a facial recognition camera pointed at the driver and alerting if the driver's eyes don't stay focused on the road ahead, or it could be a sensory element on the steering wheel that makes sure the human co-driving has their hands directly on the wheel, etc.

If you have those kinds of monitors, it would presumably decrease the risk of R3, though we don't really know as yet how much it does so.

Another factor that seems to come to play with R3 is whether there is another person in the car during a driving journey. A solo human driver that is co-sharing the driving task with the ADAS is seemingly more likely to become adrift of the driving task when alone in the car.

If there is another person in the car, perhaps one also watching the driving and urging or sparking the human driver to be attentive, it seems to prompt the human driver toward safer driving.

Rather than trying to overload the R3 or attempt to splinter the R2, let's go ahead and augment the list with this new category of the R4:

R1: Risk associated with a human driving a conventional car

R2: Risk associated with AI driving a self-driving autonomous car

R3: Risk associated with a human and AI co-sharing the driving of a car

R4: Risk associated with AI driving a self-driving car with a human back-up driver present

This leads us to these questions:

R4 < R1 ? – is AI self-driving car with human back-up driver less risky than human driven car

R4 << R1 ? -- is AI self-driving car with human back-up driver lot less risky than human driven car

Or, if you prefer:

R1 < R4 ? – is human driven car less risky than AI self-driving car with human back-up driver

R1 << R4 ? – is human driven car lot less risky than AI self-driving car with human back-up driver

We don't yet know the answer to those questions.

Indeed, some critics of the existing roadway tryouts involving self-driving cars are concerned that we are allowing a grand experiment for which we don't know what the comparative risks are.

They would assert that until there are more simulations done and closed track or proving ground efforts, these experimental self-driving cars should not be on the public roadways.

The counterargument usually voiced is that without having the self-driving cars on our public roadways it will likely delay the advent of self-driving cars, and for each day delay it is allowing by default the conventional car to continue its existing injury and death rates.

Conclusion

When someone tells you that you are taking a risk by going for a ride in a self-driving car, and assuming that there is a human back-up driver, the question is how much of a difference in risk is there between driving in a conventional car that has a human driver versus the self-driving car that has a human back-up driver.

Since you presumably are willing to accept the risk associated with being a passenger in a ridesharing car, you've already accepted some amount of risk about going onto our roadways as a rider in a car, albeit one being driven by a human.

How much more or less risk is there once you set foot into that self-driving car that has the human back-up driver?

What beguiles many critics is that the risk is not just for the riders in those self-driving cars on our public roadway.

Wherever the self-driving car roams or goes, it is opting to radiate out the risk to any nearby pedestrians and any nearby human driven cars. You don't see this imaginary radiation with your eyes, and instead it just perchance occurs because you just so happen to end-up near to one of the experimental self-driving cars on our public streets.

Are we allowing ourselves to absorb too much risk?

I'll be further contemplating this matter while ensconced in my steel vault that has protective padding and a defibrillator inside it, just in case there is an earthquake, or I have a heart murmur, or some other calamity arises.

CHAPTER 8

MAJOR PHASE SHIFT

AND

AI SELF-DRIVING CARS

CHAPTER 8

MAJOR PHASE SHIFT

AND

AI SELF-DRIVING CARS

When you are knee deep in a particular industry it can be difficult at times to notice when an overall change or shift is taking place. The day-to-day ups and downs of the industry are likely always bubbling and bumping along, thus masking to some extent any larger overarching trend.

Subtle but telling signs can inadvertently be overlooked.

In the case of the self-driving driverless car industry, I'd say that a sizable shift is underway and we are moving into a new phase.

Let's unpack my assertion.

Reading The Tea Leaves Closely

What sign or signal suggests that there is a mega phase shift occurring?

A recent announcement by General Motors (GM) that they are postponing the public roadway rollout of their autonomous car ride-hailing service was a considerable signal, though few seem to have read the tea leaves fully.

You need to consider the whole context of the matter.

First, there's the announcement itself, and secondly there is the marketplace and media reaction to the announcement.

Dan Ammann, CEO of GM Cruise (GM's self-driving driverless car entity) indicated that though they are still going full steam ahead on the tech race for achieving true autonomous cars, they assessed the status of their own efforts, carefully, thoughtfully, and have opted to delay or postpone their earlier indication that by the end of 2019 they'd be underway with commercial ride-hailing of their self-driving cars.

You might find of interest Dan Ammann's blog posting describing his assessment of their readiness and next steps (use the link here).

Within his explication, I appreciated that he mentioned something that I've been repeatedly attempting to emphasize about the self-driving car space, namely that it is a moonshot race that not only has to do with who can land on the moon first (achieve a true self-driving car), there is also the likewise vital aspect of doing so sufficiently safely enough that it garners trust among the public and all other stakeholders.

Per Ammann's comments, this is both a tech race and a trust race.

Up until now, I'd assert that many of the self-driving tech participants have overstated the tech race and grossly understated the trust race.

Using the usual tech banner of "move fast and break things," I've warned and admonished that you cannot get away with breaking things when it involves multi-ton cars on our public roadways that ultimately equate to life-and-death matters for us all.

There have been many that allowed themselves to be blinded by the "move fast" and therefore at times cut corners or rushed to put something onto the roadways that wasn't ready, or that faltered in trying to include protective measures to potentially mitigate the risks of the nascent technology.

The Uber self-driving car incident in Arizona that killed a pedestrian has served as a wake-up call for those that have this kind of tech myopia (I had prior to the incident been predicting that we all were on the precipice of something untoward happening), as have other incidents prompted similar calls, for example newsworthy incidents involving deadly Tesla car crashes, though keep in mind that Tesla's aren't (as yet) actually true autonomous cars.

Using a limited kind of analogy, we just recently celebrated the Apollo 11 moon landing, and perhaps at the same time it might be worthwhile to remember the Apollo 1 flashfire that sadly killed the crew in the cabin during a rehearsal for a launch mission. The matter caused a relook at the design and approach being used, some say it prompted a review that would have been unlikely to take place given the urgency of moving ahead in the space race.

Some might suggest that the Uber incident and other akin incidents have been a milder version of that kind of awakening.

Returning then to the GM Cruise announcement, I'd like you to notice something that was otherwise unnoticed.

Ask yourself this question: What happened as a result of the announcement?

Well, it was pretty much taken in stride by the marketplace and the media.

Headlines about the matter were relatively muted, mainly just pointing out that there was a delay in the projected launch date for the commercial ride-hailing service with their self-driving cars. Analysts were composed and offered commentary that was filled with aspects declaring that they weren't necessarily surprised and that it was nothing to get riled about.

Furthermore, on the day of the announcement, the stock of GM closed at $40.88, ending on an slight tick up basis by about 0.4%.

Why The Reaction Was The Tell

By now you are probably wondering why I am seemingly pointing out the "obvious" aspects about the response to the GM Cruise announcement, all of which you perchance noticed in your daily news feeds.

Here's why I bring it up.

The announcement did not result in the (usual) our "world is going to end" proclamations.

Remember how it used to be that any indication of even the slightest delay or postponement by a self-driving car maker was heralded as a disgrace for that firm?

You might as well have committed hari-kari if you were the top executive of an automaker or tech firm that even whispered that you were undertaking a delay in something related to your autonomous car efforts.

In fact, top leaders in the self-driving car space quickly learned that it was politically incorrect to use words like "delay" or "postpone," any of which was an immediate red flag, no matter what it was that was being actually delayed or postponed.

The stock price of the offending firm would almost instantly take a painful hit when such announcements were made.

The viewpoint of the marketplace was that any firm that wasn't striding at the utmost pace was going to lose this vaunted tech race. The littlest stumble or appearance of a stumble meant that your firm was falling behind, and such a faltering could not be tolerated, not one iota.

Some top execs lost their jobs because they didn't appear to be taking self-driving cars seriously enough or they weren't riding herd on their driverless car efforts with sufficient bluster and urgency.

I'm trying to bring your attention then to what didn't happen upon GM Cruise making its announcement. It is easy to observe what did happen, while it takes some out-of-the-box thinking to consider what didn't happen.

Here's the skinny:

What did happen is the stock price of GM stayed about the same and actually blipped up, while what did not happen is the stock suffering a beating due to the indicated delay in their self-driving car commercialization efforts.

What did happen is that the media presented the matter as a relatively mild announcement, while what did not happen was a massive castigating of the firm for the open admission of a delay.

What did happen was Ammann got mainly subtle approvals by the marketplace for being forthcoming, while what did not happen was a rebuke or name calling as to his publicly making known the delay.

What did happen was that analysts chimed in and said that this is an emerging and taken in-stride pattern and we all should expect more of it, while what did not happen was a sky-is-falling headline grabbing series of proclamations that self-driving cars are never going to work and investors should flee at once from these efforts.

Conclusion

Overall, I attribute the willingness of GM Cruise to make the announcement as an indicator that they and Ammann anticipated that they could be forthright and transparent without having to take the usually expected slings and arrows.

Their willingness to make the announcement, coupled with the resulting calm response by the marketplace and the media, would have been unfathomable previously.

The self-driving car industry is in the midst of a phase shift, I suggest.

Gradually, the mania of the madcap tech race is giving way to a balance with the trust race. The mantra of "move fast and break things" is giving way to "move fast and do it right."

Don't though misinterpret my remarks to suggest the tech race is somehow lessened or put on a backburner. Heavens no. The tech race is still rocketing ahead.

What I am saying is that the trust race is now finally entering more formidably into the picture. Many that were willing previously to assume that if some eggs got broken it was okay and essentially part-and-parcel of trying to get to a true autonomous car first, they are now realizing that maybe they'll need to rethink that equation.

Of course, there are going to be some in the self-driving car space that might be desperate enough that they would over-emphasize the tech race and underplay the trust race. Not everyone in this arena is going to be balancing these factors in the same way.

Overall, when looked at across the board for the self-driving car industry as a whole, it seems to me that we have entered into a next phase consisting of two intertwined and inseparable factors, tech and trust.

As a warning for those that don't see the intertwining or won't embrace the intertwining, they are going to find themselves out-of-step and likely no longer have the prior over-the-top mania to serve as a cover for driverless cars efforts that wantonly subjugate the trust race to the tech race.

CHAPTER 9

LEVEL 3 TECH MISGIVINGS FOR SMART CARS

CHAPTER 9
LEVEL 3 TECH MISGIVINGS
FOR SMART CARS

We are entering into a murky driving era involving semi-autonomous cars, ones that are not yet proficient at true self-driving and are intended as an ADAS (Advanced Driver-Assistance System) capability only.

Don't mistakenly confuse these Level 3 cars with the fully autonomous Level 4 and Level 5 self-driving driverless cars that are being devised and tested.

In the case of Level 3, the human driver is co-sharing the driving task with the automation of the car, yet, nonetheless, you, as the human driver remain undeniably the responsible party for the driving of the vehicle. You cannot try to hope or pretend that the automation is the driver, since it is decidedly not the true driver, and you must at all times realize that you are the accountable driver sitting at the wheel of the car.

I've predicted that as the ADAS automation improves, it will lull human drivers into a sense of complacency about the driving task. This is regrettable, dangerous, and playing with fire in terms of what it portends for driving on our roadways.

Right now, we all reasonably know that the everyday automation on a conventional car is too rudimentary to do much of any of the driving task, therefore we tend to keep our attention riveted toward driving the car. In a kind of irony, the more that the ADAS automation improves, it essentially fools you into falsely believing it can drive the car, when the actual fact is that it cannot, and you must remain just as vigilant as ever.

Worrisome too is that the media keeps fanning the flames associated with advances in ADAS automation. Those that don't fully grasp what is going on are apt to gush about any new features that are announced about ADAS. Yes, it is certainly handy and significant that ADAS continues to improve, yet in the same breath it is important to point out the potential "gap" this will create between what drivers need to do and what they mistakenly will fall prey to doing.

I'd like to use the recent announcement of Nissan's ProPILOT 2.0 as an exemplar of my points about how we all need to take a breath and calmly consider how Level 3 is going to impact our driving and the nature of what takes place on our highways and byways.

I'm not going to refer to Level 3 cars as "self-driving" since I believe this to be a misleading moniker. I would wager that most people assume that something that can "self-drive" is able to autonomously drive a car, doing so without any human intervention needed. The same qualms apply to the phrases of "driverless cars" and for "autonomous cars," all of which suggests the AI can drive the car itself, and for which I reserve those phrases for Level 4 and Level 5 vehicles.

Level 3 cars are semi-autonomous, at best, meaning they have some autonomy-like capabilities and can aid or augment what a human driver is doing. They are not autonomous.

Also, though I am focusing in this instance on the Nissan ProPILOT 2.0, please realize that my commentary applies to all the other emerging Level 3 cars too. It's going to be an across-the-board matter that encompasses any and all Level 3 vehicles.

Recent Announcement About Nissan ProPILOT 2.0

You likely already know that Nissan has offered the ProPILOT Assist since about 2016 and it has been around for several years now.

The ADAS capability of ProPILOT Assist includes aspects such as adaptive cruise control, along with a lane centering feature, and several other subsystems to mildly augment the human driver. Those features when first introduced were somewhat novel and uncommon, and since then have become essentially part-and-parcel of most modern-day cars.

The newest incarnation of the ProPILOT is labeled as version 2.0.

It's the usual leapfrog aspects of tech on cars.

An automaker comes up with something relatively new, brings it to the marketplace, others are doing the same to compete, and eventually the innovation becomes the new norm. This then prompts the automakers to try and rejigger the game by coming out with even newer features, and the cycle of those capabilities ultimately becoming the norm then repeats itself over and over.

The ProPILOT 2.0 will reportedly be available in Japan initially and then eventually be made available in other markets including the United States.

One small aspect that I'd like to note.

I had welcomed that the ProPILOT Assist had purposely been named to include the word "Assist" when it was first coined by Nissan, doing so by their own awareness that some of the names of ADAS systems are misleading and imply greater capability than truly provided (there is an ongoing and acrimonious debate about Tesla using the word "Autopilot"). By having added the word "Assist" to the ProPILOT name, it hopefully clued drivers that the system was only of an assisting nature.

I bring this up because so far it appears that ProPILOT 2.0 might not contain the word "Assist" and if so, it to me seems like an unfortunate dropping of a word that at least attempted to recognize the limited aspects of being semi-autonomous.

I realize you can argue that maybe people don't pay attention to the names of things anyway, and so perhaps it is inconsequential how you name these systems, but I don't buy into that argument and assert that the name does still make a difference.

In any case, the ProPILOT 2.0 includes upgrades to the sensory devices used for the ADAS, including improved cameras and radar and sonar units, mounted around the car to try and achieve a 360-degree perspective, plus a new 3D HD (High Definition) mapping data and GPS subsystem, an eyes-on feature, and some other added capabilities.

It is being suggested and stated that these new features will allow for hands-off driving in certain circumstances.

I won't go into the details herein about the situations that allow you to presumably go hands-off, trying to keep this piece somewhat brief, and am going to focus more so on the overall notion of allowing for and encouraging hands-off related driving.

How Eyes-On And Hands-Off Are Problematic

The media has reacted to the ProPILOT 2.0 announcement with some rather breathless claims, such as:

"Truly hands-free auto-navigating highway driving" – this is grossly misleading, there are crucial limits to when the hands-free or hands-off driving is intended to be used

"Eye-scanning tech makes certain the driver is paying attention to the road" – a false statement in that the eye-scanning or eyes-on can help increase the chances of the driver paying attention to the driving task but it is far from being a certainty

Allow me a moment to elaborate about why the eyes-on and hands-off proposition is quite unsettling.

With eyes-on, a car has an inward facing camera pointed at your face and eyes, which is then used to try and detect if your head is facing toward the road and also detect if your eyes are aimed ahead too. Some systems only detect the position of your head, some detect only the position of your eyes, while most of these kinds of systems are converging toward detecting both your head position and your eyes position.

If you turn your head toward say a passenger seated next to your driver's position, the system would detect that your head has turned away and would alert you. Likewise, if your eyes shift to look downward at the speedometer of your car, the system can usually detect that your eyes are no longer looking forward and will alert you accordingly. These systems tend to allow you to avert your gaze or shift your head momentarily, thus not instantaneously barking at you all of the time.

Some seem to think that as long as you are keeping your eyes aimed at the road ahead, this allows you to then remove your hands from the steering wheel, since presumably you are still paying attention to the driving task and it is merely the seemingly inconsequential matter that your hands aren't on the steering wheel anymore.

Thus, by having a built-in system to try and ensure that your eyes remain riveted ahead, we are entering into this new territory of Level 3 cars that will increasingly tout that you no longer have to grasp your steering wheel.

I ask you, what will you do with your hands-off ability?

If you have the freedom to do whatever you want with your hands, it seems doubtful that you'll keep them at-the-ready near the steering wheel. I'd bet that you would use your hands to hold that coffee cup or grab an item from the backseat of the car or help your child that's seated next to you.

Your hands will now become adrift of the driving task, more so than ever before. And, whereas you might have kept one hand on the steering wheel, allowing the other hand to do the kinds of actions I've just mentioned, now you'll be taking both hands off the wheel.

There are three key factors about your hands:

- Time
- Distance
- Grasping

Let's explore the three factors by considering a driving activity.

You are driving on the freeway. A car ahead of you suddenly hits its brakes. You can try to hit your brakes too, or possibly swerve your car to avoid a crash. The act of swerving your car is going to require that your hands be on the steering wheel, doing so to turn the wheel in whichever direction seems best to swerve and to the degree that you need to swerve to avoid the accident.

With eyes-on tech, I'll pretend that you are watching the road ahead and see the car that's suddenly braking.

Meanwhile, your hands were both entirely off the steering wheel. Your left-hand was fiddling with the seat adjustment knob, since you were trying to reposition the driver's seat for more comfort, and your right-hand was being used to hold a sippy cup for your young child next to you.

Upon the startling realization that the car ahead is coming to a tire screeching halt, you need to take your left hand off the seat adjustment knob, move your left arm and left hand so that the hand becomes closer to the steering wheel, and then grab the steering wheel with your now available left hand.

Your right hand presumably is simultaneously dropping the sippy cup, and your right arm and right hand are repositioning closer to the steering wheel, eventually allowing your right hand to now be positioned on the wheel and cooperate with your left hand.

How long does that take to happen?

I'll be generous and say that it takes just 2-3 seconds, though you might want to consult my review of various research studies about the reaction times of human drivers and how sluggish us humans can be. At a speed of around 70 miles per hour, those 2-3 seconds means that you've traveled about 200 to 300 feet, perhaps nearly the length of a football field.

You might have struck that car ahead of you in the time it takes to get your hands onto the wheel.

Or, your options of swerving might no longer exist because of the delay in turning the wheel. And so on.

Thus, by having your hands-off, you are tempting fate in terms of the time it will require to get your hands back onto the wheel and in a usable posture, which is also impacted by the distance that your hands were from the wheel, along with whatever might have been in your hands that you were grasping at the time that you needed them for purposes of being on the wheel.

I don't believe that the eyes-on gives you the ultimate freedom of being hands-off, especially not when you are driving a Level 3 car that depends upon you as the human driver to take over the driving task, something that you never actually could or should give away to start with, since you are still the responsible party driving the car.

The Human Driving Elements Being Reconsidered

With the Level 3 cars, we are starting to mix-and-match the following possibilities:

- Eyes-on versus eyes-off

- Hands-on versus hands-off

- Feet-on versus feet-off

- Mind-on driving versus mind-off driving

Apparently, you can seemingly pick selections from the list and match them as you might so wish to do.

This seems highly questionable for ADAS and Level 3 driving.

I'd like to assert some rules of human driving that seem pertinent:

The more of your sensory apparatus that are "off" the driving task, the worse it will be when you need those to urgently control the car

Your eyes-on does not guarantee that you are fully engaged in the driving task, since you mind can still be elsewhere, especially if it is dealing with your hands-off or feet-off aspects

The shifting of your sensory apparatus to being "off" the driving task will exacerbate the likelihood of your mind going adrift too

Here's something else that seems equally worrisome.

Will human drivers that are less capable at driving become emboldened to drive when they otherwise would not have been driving, since they now come to believe that the ADAS Level 3 is going to make-up for any of their own driving deficiencies or foibles?

Think about drunk drivers.

Consider too the nature of novice teenage drivers.

Those teenage budding drivers are statistically already in a high-risk category of driving, partially due to their inexperience at driving and also at times due to being easily distracted from the driving task. If they are driving a car that allows them the latitude of being hands-off, will this even worsen their plight and the plight of the rest of us that come near to those cars?

You could claim that the eyes-on feature might actually help reduce car accidents by those novice teenage drivers because it will be a means to presumably force them to remain focused on the road ahead. Yes, this might be partially the case, though remember that it is allowing for them to correspondingly remove their hands-off the wheel, which would seem to counter-balance or undermine the benefits of the eyes-on.

Conclusion

For systems designers, it is a common understanding that humans generally flow like water to whatever is the least they need to do for a given task at-hand.

The eyes-on is helpful, and we ought to also note that Level 3 cars that lack eyes-on are in a worse status than those that are arming their cars with eyes-on.

The hands-off is potentially alarming since it is taking us inch-by-inch toward becoming less engaged in the driving task, which for Level 3 is disconcerting.

I've repeatedly predicted that we are going to have a slew of lawsuits down-the-road about these matters.

If you get hit by a Level 3 car that the driver had their hands-off the wheel, doing so by the encouragement of the automaker or tech firm, it seems likely you and your attorney will go after the car designer for having setup what could be construed as a powder keg ready to someday explode.

For the moment, we can expect a myriad of Level 3 designs and approaches to enter into the marketplace, coming onto our roadways as part of a grand experiment, seeing how far we can stretch the human driving act toward becoming a field of actually driving the car, and yet meanwhile assuming or expecting that the human driver is supposedly driving the car.

Watch out.

CHAPTER 10

PRESIDENTIAL DEBATE

LESSONS

AND

AI SELF-DRIVING CARS

CHAPTER 10

PRESIDENTIAL DEBATE LESSONS
AND
AI SELF-DRIVING CARS

The 2019 Democratic Presidential Debate is now in the history books, having come and gone, and has been roundly examined, analyzed, probed, scrutinized and scoured for all kinds of signs and tweets about what happened and what it all means.

I'd like to take a moment and see what we might glean as lessons learned that could be recast into the emerging arena of self-driving driverless cars.

Your first thought might be that you don't recall anybody on the stage last week in either of the two nights of debates having mentioned self-driving cars.

Yes, you would be right in not having heard the catchphrases of driverless cars or autonomous cars or self-driving cars uttered in the at-times acrimonious debating points that came up during those two invigorating nights.

And, sensibly, there'd be no particular reason at this time that it would have become a topic of discussion in the tightly timed deliberations which focused on today's major societal concerns.

I would though like to make a prediction.

If any of the existing self-driving car efforts that are undertaking public roadway testing happen to encounter a crash and death such as the Uber incident in Phoenix of last year, and if this happens close in time to the upcoming further Democratic Presidential debates, it could indeed then become a topic of attention at those debates.

Let's hope that doesn't happen.

In any case, I'll also make the claim that for the 2024 race for presidency we will almost certainly have the topic of self-driving cars being included into the presidential debates at that time.

My basis for such a seemingly bold or maybe out-of-the-blue claim is that we'll likely have a greater prominence of self-driving cars as we enter into the early 2020's, and by the time we get to 2024 there are bound to be a slew of issues that have appeared due to the initial emergence of autonomous cars onto our roadways in a larger scale. Besides the possibilities of deaths and injuries, we'll undoubtedly be mired in political and societal disputes about how much free rein the autonomous cars ought to have and what we're all going to do about the mixing of human driven cars and driverless cars.

There won't be any free lunch when it comes to the advent of self-driving cars.

Contentious and thorny issues will ultimately arise and be difficult to resolve.

Putting aside that somewhat gloomy or downcast looking future, let's get back to the recent debates.

You can interpret last week's debates in an out-of-the-box way, namely by considering how the various key debating positions were raised and discussed, including how the candidates staked-out a position or attacked another candidate or tried to rebuff an attack.

Let's unpack those aspects.

Key Debating Elements Recast For Self-Driving Cars

I've tried to eke out the underlying debate-related tactics that the candidates utilized and have then pointed out how the same thinking is applicable to today's self-driving car deliberations.

Here you go:

- Being Wonky Can Lose Your Audience

Presidential Debate: There were some in-depth and wonky kinds of debating about the arcane aspects of healthcare, which left some of the general public unsure of what the candidates positions actually consisted of.

Self-Driving Cars: Automakers and tech firms sometimes provide highly technical explanations about what they are doing in terms of developing and fielding of self-driving cars, doing so in a manner that only industry insiders can comprehend, leaving the general public and regulators unsure what the industry is undertaking.

- Sound Bites Are Catchy

Presidential Debate: The candidates either prepared catchy sound bites or perchance landed on catchy sound bites, though sometimes the sound bite used didn't get the impact that the candidate necessarily wanted. Either way, sound bites tended to dominate much of the post-debate talking points.

Self-Driving Cars: The use of sound bites to express the alleged wonderment of self-driving cars has not yet especially caught on, but you can bet that the marketing side of the automakers and tech firms will come up with some grabbers and use those with glee. There is a touch of this already taking place for the ads of the upcoming Level 3 semi-autonomous cars.

- Sound Bits Often Are Misleading

Presidential Debate: Though some of the sound bites voiced were memorable, including about cool-aid and also about yada-yada-yada, ultimately becoming widespread viral attention getters, several of the expressed phrases were labeled by some as misleading and lacking in substance.

Self-Driving Cars: You can bet your bottom dollar that the automakers and tech firms are going to be providing sound bites that are misleading. There is already an ongoing and fierce debate about whether Tesla's use of the word "Autopilot" is an overreach and misleads drivers into relying excessively on the automation of the car. Expect much more of these kinds of problematic wording issues as we get closer to reality for self-driving cars.

- Attacking Each Other Can Be Mutual Destruction

Presidential Debate: Talking heads have said that the candidates might have done damage upon themselves by attacking each other, rather than focusing on others that might have been affronted. This has been likened as a form of Mutually Assured Destruction (MAD) in a debating forum of this kind.

Self-Driving Cars: When the commercial aspects of self-driving cars first got underway, there were attacks aplenty of startups that said the big automakers were behind-the-times and asleep at the wheel. There were even ferocious attacks among the startups themselves as to which had the better strategy or had the golden egg that would magically make self-driving cars appear overnight. This didn't seem to help the industry at the time. Subsequently, the industry has become generally civil and polite toward each other, though Elon Musk stands out as being more (shall we say) undiplomatic about the competition.

- Prior Views Can Boomerang On You

Presidential Debate: In the first round of debates, one candidate scored mightily by using a prior position of another candidate. For the second round of debates, it seemed as though nearly all of the candidates tried to arm themselves with excerpted prior positions that could be lunged into the body politic of another candidate like a sabre or epee strike.

Self-Driving Cars: We've certainly had quite a number of automakers and tech firms that had earlier predicted that by today we'd all be joyfully riding around in our fully Level 5 autonomous cars. Not so. Not even close. The media trots out those predictions from time-to-time but has actually been rather gentile about using it against anyone. One position that will become perhaps the most likely to garner attention will be Elon Musk's positions on LIDAR, which he has unequivocally denounced, and we'll all need to wait-and-see how that one turns out.

- Use Your Own Strength As Your Attack Vector

Presidential Debate: During the debate, some of the candidates would attempt to switch the topic at-hand and move onto a topic that they believed was in their own best interest, allowing them to not only showcase their strength, it also permitted them to then attack other candidates from an "attack vector" (angle) best suited to their own campaign. This is pretty much a typical and often used debate tactic for anyone versed in speech-and-debate strategies.

Self-Driving Cars: If you look closely, you can see mild undertones of this kind of showmanship in the self-driving car industry, whereby some automaker or tech firm will emphasize say highway driving over inner city driving (because they have concentrated on highway driving), or maybe brag about a certain kind of sensor that they've focused their own efforts on. Let's use Tesla again, simply because they've been quite outspoken and assert that they've got lots of camera related data stored in their cars and their cloud that they suggest gives them a huge advantage over others, though this is somewhat arguable (for more about this notion, see my article here).

- Make-Up A Question Vs Answer The Actual Question

Presidential Debate: Another popular debate tactic involves trying to avoid the question that was asked of you, and instead provide an "answer" for a question that you made-up and that wasn't actually asked of you. For example, when asked about a crime bill, a candidate might shift into saying how crime is absolutely abhorrent (thus, not replying directly about the crime bill, and deflecting to a safer question of whether crime is a good thing or a bad thing), or perhaps start talking about education (a matter related to crime overall, but not specific to the question about the crime bill).

Self-Driving Cars: We are right now faced with having self-driving cars on our public roadways in a form of unacknowledged public experiment, and for which even with a human back-up driver there are still clear-cut risks involved to us all. During industry presentations, some pundits favoring this approach have at times tried to shift the question at-hand and instead discuss how great the world will be once self-driving cars are widely available. Though that might be the case, we all still need to consider the risks we are embracing today for that hoped-for future.

Conclusion

I hope you enjoyed the walk down "memory lane" about last week's debate.

Only a week has passed and yet it seems that the fleeting attention of the media has put the debate into the can, awaiting being reopened once we get closer to the next round of debates. The media will open the sealed can at that time, prying it from the collective recesses of our minds, and try to use it as grist for what the candidates might do in their latest round.

By the way, please don't interpret my analysis about the Democratic debates as somehow any different in terms of debating tactics and ploys that you would see in the Republican debates.

There's no question that if you look back at the Republican debates for the presidential election in 2016, you'd see the same kind of efforts. I am merely citing the Democratic debates herein since they are fresh in all of our minds.

Put aside the Democratic or Republican aspects and instead look at what I was really trying to discuss. I wanted to bring up the debates that we aren't yet fully having about self-driving cars, and yet for which we will eventually and inexorably need to have.

Perhaps my comments will help get you ready for that day.

CHAPTER 11

CLOUD BREECHES

AND

AI SELF-DRIVING CARS

CHAPTER 11

CLOUD BREECHES

AND

AI SELF-DRIVING CARS

The news has been covering yet another breech of systems security that involves the pilfering of massive amounts of data, in this case impacting an estimated 100 million customers of Capital One bank.

In the past, the public might have reacted vociferously in outright dismay and disgust.

Nowadays, these kinds of revelations seem to happen regularly and so people are irked and exasperated, but not storming the castle gates of the companies that let this happen.

Interestingly, the companies are able to somehow portray themselves as a victim, gaining sympathy at times, having been presumably outfoxed by (one assumes) sinister hackers that must have divine superpowers to crack into Fort Knox.

Furthermore, these intruded-upon companies are usually well-prepared to rush forward to aid those that were impacted, often consisting of simply covering a credit monitoring subscription for some length of time, along with taking on any financial hit in subsequent lawsuits.

As someone that used to be deeply involved in cybersecurity, including having done consulting work and spoken at major industry events, I had said then and continue to repeat today that by-and-large firms are not devoting sufficient resources and attention to cybersecurity.

In fact, firms pretty much know they avoid doing so, betting that the costs associated with a breech impact will be less than the upfront costs toward truly extensive preventative system security efforts.

Which is worse, paying now with dollars that you could use for other purposes, or paying once or if a cybersecurity breech befalls you?

The math seems to sway toward mildly putting effort toward cybersecurity today and hoping that the hacked future will not arise (or possibly occur on someone else's watch).

If society opted to shun the firms that allowed these breeches to occur, the overall cost to the companies would be large enough that they would take a more somber tone and more generous allotment toward their systems security.

There is also what I refer to as the earthquake phenomena.

A lot of firms don't consider themselves fully at risk of a cybersecurity breech, just as a lot of homeowners don't think their house is vulnerable to being wrecked by an earthquake. And, even if earthquakes harm other houses, the homeowner that believes they won't be harmed will cling to not getting earthquake insurance.

Cloud Attention

This latest earthquake-like cybersecurity incident with Capital One has prompted the media to twist things more so than usual.

In this case, Capital One had earlier famously embraced moving off of their own hardware and into the cloud, making a large-scale deal with Amazon's AWS cloud services, doing so in a loud and bragging manner, taking a stand that many in the industry were still unsure of equally making.

Many financial institutions have been queasy about moving away from their own bought and managed platforms, since they worried about whether the cloud would be secure enough.

I have pointed out to companies unsure about adopting an external cloud service that one of the potential benefits is that the cloud service company potentially has hordes of cybersecurity specialists that have as their mainstay the protection of their overall cloud systems. An individual firm would be unlikely to command such a large force devoted to such security, while the cloud service provider can do so since they are needing to secure the overarching cloud capability across all of their clients (in a sense, spreading out their cybersecurity costs).

There is a rub though.

You have to make sure you differentiate the so-called "security of the cloud" versus the "security in the cloud."

The cloud provider typically states that they have primary responsibility for security of the cloud, meaning that the cloud system or platform is kept relatively secure by the cloud provider, and less so is a responsibility of the company using the cloud service.

Meanwhile, security in the cloud means that the company using the cloud service has the primary responsibility of making sure they are using the cloud platform in a secure manner, and this is less so a requirement of the cloud provider.

Translated, this implies that a locksmith will try to make sure that your home has a good lock on the front door (that's the cloud provider as the "security of the cloud"), but if you leave the house key laying under the doormat it's your fault for undermining the security of the home (that's the company using the cloud and having usurped their role of "security in the cloud").

According to news reports to-date, allegedly Capital One did not adequately configure the use of their AWS provided cloud service.

If that's the case, one could argue that it was a misstep of security in the cloud rather than security of the cloud.

Sometimes these matters devolve into a finger pointing match.

A company might say that they thought the cloud provider was doing this-or-that, and therefore the company didn't need to do so. Or, a company might complain that the cloud provider didn't sufficiently warn them about needing to do certain configurations or was lax in not letting the company know that existing configurations were weak.

These co-shared responsibilities can become an inadvertent gap in cybersecurity.

A famous line in cybersecurity is that a company has to be right all of the time (always protected), while the crook or hacker only has to be "right" once (finding a hole and then exploiting it right away).

Applies To AI Self-Driving Cars

Let's shift our attention away from clouds that contain banking data to instead discuss clouds that contain other kinds of data.

Specifically, consider the role of clouds in the advent of self-driving driverless cars.

A self-driving car typically has lots of sensors, including cameras, radar, ultrasonic, LIDAR, and so on. These sensors are collecting vast amounts of data. The data normally goes into the on-board systems and electronic memory of the driverless car.

Pretty quickly, the volume of data gets large.

The AI system driving the car generally needs live data at the time the data is collected and doesn't need prior data quite as much. That being said, the prior or previously collected data can be a treasure trove for doing Machine Learning and Deep Learning, allowing the AI system to improve its driving capabilities over time by analyzing and "learning" from the amassed data.

Keeping that data on-board a specific car is not going to leverage it entirely, thus, most of the automakers and tech firms push the data up to a cloud.

The cloud could be a homegrown platform by the automaker or tech firm, or it might be an externally provided cloud service (similar to how Capital One selected an outside cloud provider).

If you sense where I'm going on this, yes, I'm suggesting that ultimately there will be tons of data collected from our self-driving cars and this data will be housed in clouds somewhere.

Suppose a hacker breaks into a cloud that houses the sensory data collected from your own self-driving car.

So what?

Essentially, the hacker could likely figure out where you went, how long you stayed there, how many trips you made per day, and so on. This might seem innocent and seemingly inconsequential, but it could allow the hacker to target you by knowing where you go. Other nefarious uses that I won't even mention herein come to mind too.

Furthermore, it is anticipated that self-driving cars will likely have an inward facing camera, doing so to catch people being disruptive in self-driving ride-sharing cars, and there will be audio capabilities too such as a microphone allowing you to interact with the AI system (akin to Alexa or Siri).

Assume that every car journey that you've made is recorded on video and audio and sitting in the cloud of the automaker or tech firm.

Does this seem to disturb you a little bit more about the potential for privacy invasion?

As an aside, I'm focusing in this discussion on the possibility of your data being leaked or stolen by a hacker. Keep in mind that the automaker or tech firm might choose to use that collected data, perhaps to do marketing campaigns aimed at your ascertained interests or might sell the data to third parties that want to use it for various purposes.

Thus, we all still have yet to confront the matter of how data about you, collected via self-driving cars, will be utilized and whether you will be allowed to have any control over the collection and distribution of such private data.

Moving Beyond Read-Only

One aspect about having self-driving car data in the cloud involves it being seen by a hacker and then copied from the official cloud site to some other online hacker-preferred location.

In theory, the hacker might be able to get not only the automaker or tech firm cloud-stored data but even seek to get the official cloud to request additional data from the self-driving car itself.

Therefore, beyond simply picking up data already pushed from the self-driving car up to the cloud, it could be that the hacker invokes the cloud to grab data from the driverless car, either new data that had not yet made its way to the cloud or possibly even other data that the automaker or tech firm had not envisioned would be pushed up to the cloud.

I'll next move into even scarier waters.

The cloud transmissions are often referred to as OTA (Over The Air) electronic communications. OTA is used to grab data from the self-driving cars and place it into the cloud.

Plus, OTA is used to push data and even programs down into the self-driving car.

Here's where we veer into a potential nightmare.

If a hacker can get the cloud to push down data that might confuse or mislead the AI of the self-driving car, in theory the hacker could potentially get the car to go places or do things that the hacker desires.

Similarly, if the OTA is normally providing routine updates to executable programs that are on-board the AI system of the driverless car, the hacker could try to put their own hijacked program into the self-driving car, doing so readily without having to get physical access to the self-driving car.

In that manner, the OTA is a dual-edged sword. It is helpful and handy for self-driving cars since it allows for remote updates to be applied to the AI system, yet it also provides a nifty and convenient conduit to allow a hacker to do some reprehensible things.

It is noteworthy that particular automakers or tech firms will have fleets of self-driving cars. A hacker would possibly be able to infect an entire fleet, doing so via the OTA, and do this without breaking a sweat, having the OTA transmit to all of the self-driving cars wherever they might be on planet earth.

Ironically, I suppose, the fact that to-date each of the automakers and tech firms are generally using separate and proprietary clouds means that a hacker couldn't necessarily hack all driverless cars per se. To do so, the hacker would have to crack into each of the distinct clouds of the various automakers and tech firms. This would be harder, though still possible.

Conclusion

Having dragged you through the cloud aspects of self-driving cars, my point is that the same kind of breeching action that happened to Capital One and to lots of other companies could also happen to self-driving car companies.

The potential loss of privacy is certainly serious in the case of online banking break-ins, and the same could happen with self-driving car data, but I think we can all agree that the danger is ratcheted up if the hacking can potentially impact the driving of a car.

A myriad of doomsday scenarios has already been voiced that a hacker might decide to stop all traffic in a given city and cause a swirl of calamity. There are of course even worse scenarios to consider.

Right now, though the self-driving car companies are providing some attention to cybersecurity, they really aren't much of an attractive target as yet by hackers. Until we have a lot of driverless cars on the roads, it just isn't as magnetic a pull for hackers to go after this arena.

The number of cybersecurity holes or avenues for hacking are enormous for driverless cars.

Besides the cloud connection, there is also the possibility of Internet of Things (IoT) devices that might be inside or near to a self-driving car that can create security issues. The infotainment systems inside a driverless car provide a platform for launching a hacking attack upon the car. Even your smartphone, carried with you when you go into a self-driving car for a driving journey, it too can be a springboard for making an attack.

Step further back and consider the entire supply chain related to making a car. Throughout that supply chain, something can potentially be implanted that would allow for an electronic opening once the self-driving car is on our roadways.

I realize that some might be upset that I've seemingly been saying that the sky is falling. The focus of the automakers is primarily on getting their self-driving cars to work, and we don't yet know how well guarded those systems are.

Cybersecurity in the case of autonomous cars must be given top priority, else we'll be discussing later on that though we did achieve driverless cars, and assume they are safe as drivers, they might be unsafe due to the chances that a hacker might decide to create their own kind of earthquake.

CHAPTER 12

THE MORAL IMPERATIVE

AND

AI SELF-DRIVING CARS

CHAPTER 12
THE MORAL IMPERATIVE
AND
AI SELF-DRIVING CARS

Some have been saying that the advent of self-driving cars is a moral imperative.

Most notable of the prognosticators about driverless cars and someone that simultaneously leverages the vaunted moral imperative moniker would undoubtedly be Elon Musk, doing so as an explication of his efforts at Tesla. He's not the only one saying so, and there are plenty of others that also have used that expression of faith or belief in the future for self-driving cars.

What though does it actually mean to assert that the goal of achieving self-driving driverless cars is in fact a moral imperative?

Let's unpack the claim.

Defining Self-Driving Driverless Cars

If there is going to be a moral imperative about something, we ought to first at least agree on what the something is, otherwise the discussion or argument about the moral imperative will be meandering and confounded.

As such, I'd like to take a moment and clarify the meaning of self-driving driverless cars.

There are semi-autonomous cars that require a human driver that co-shares in the driving effort, typically referred to as a Level 2 and a Level 3 car. I don't consider those kinds of cars to be truly self-driving driverless cars because they require a human driver.

For me, I'm somewhat literal and believe that the phrase "self-driving" and the word "driverless" each suggest that the car drives itself, entirely, solely, done exclusively by an AI system, and for which there is no human driver involved at all. This would be considered a Level 5 car, and somewhat a Level 4 car though the Level 4 is limited in ways that don't make it fully autonomous in an entirely unrestricted way (it is constrained by whatever an automaker defines as its ODD's or Operational Design Domains).

In terms of a moral imperative, I believe that most would agree that the presumed moral imperative they are alluding to pertains to achieving fully autonomous cars, those of the Level 5 and to some degree the Level 4.

I suppose there are some that might want to extend the moral imperative to encompass the semi-autonomous cars too. You might press for such a case by arguing that if the automation on a semi-autonomous car gets better and better, it will presumably make the human co-driving the car to be a "better" driver too due to the augmentation by the automation.

As I've previously laid out, none of us yet know whether or not the augmentation by automation is going to turnout well. It could be that the advanced automation in say Level 3 cars leads to human co-drivers that become lulled into being adrift of the driving task, and when push comes to shove, and an urgency arises in the driving task, the human driver might not respond promptly and thus actually be a worse driver than if they were driving unaided by the automation.

Nobody can yet say how it will go, and we are entering into a massive experiment on our public roadways as a society with the emerging Level 3 cars.

In any case, let's focus our attention about the moral imperative toward the advent of true self-driving driverless cars that are fully autonomous and there is no element of a human driver involved.

Moral Imperative Basis

Having defined the focus of the moral imperative, namely fully autonomous cars, we next ought to consider what does a moral imperative itself consist of.

If you want to be somewhat philosophical, you could hark back to the writings of Immanuel Kant in the 1780's that attempted to define mankind's sense of morality.

Generally, he suggested that a moral imperative would be a proposition by mankind that a particular action or possibly an inaction was a necessity for mankind. This would be a moral imperative as it either was supported by reasoning or logic, or instead it might be a divine aspect of our creation and our special place in the world, possibly going beyond any discernable semblance of reasoning per se and instead might simply be a defacto part of humanity.

Rather than getting stuck in the weeds of whether or not the "moral imperative" for the achievement of true self-driving driverless cars is a divine aspect, I'll tackle herein the assumption that the moral imperative arises by some kind of logical basis or argument.

Okay, so then what is the logical basis that underlies the assertion that there is a moral imperative for the fully autonomous car emergence?

The logical basis appears to consist of these tenets:

- Elimination of human fatalities and injuries due to cars

The biggest, boldest, and most oft mentioned of the moral argument tenets is that self-driving driverless cars will eliminate all human fatalities and injuries that today arise from the use of conventional cars.

If this was indeed a valid assertion, it pretty much argues vehemently for the need to get us to fully autonomous cars, saving the 40,000 lives lost each year in the United States alone and sparing us the approximately 2.5 million or more injuries in the U.S. due to car accidents (note that the numbers would be much higher in terms of lives saved and injuries avoided if based on worldwide counts).

You could then say that it has to be an "imperative" and one that we would seek to achieve as soon as possible, since seemingly any delay in trying to achieve this moral tenet would mean that lives are being needlessly lost.

Unfortunately, the argument is not so neatly simplified and there are valid counterpoints to be considered.

First, you can forget about the notion of zero fatalities and zero injuries in an era of self-driving driverless cars. If a pedestrian darts into the street from between two parked cars, and the self-driving driverless car is coming down the street at the posted speed limit of say 40 miles per hour, the physics of the situation belies the self-driving car of magically stopping in time. The same could be said about a bicyclist that suddenly veers into the path of a self-driving car. And so on.

In addition, there is an implied assumption that self-driving driverless cars are going to be perfect drivers that always will be infallible in their driving efforts. This belies the possibility of latent bugs or errors in the AI driving system. This belies the possibility of AI system failures that arise and for which the system gets out-of-whack and no longer is driving the car as prescribed.

And another twist is that we are going to have human driven cars mixing with AI driven fully autonomous cars, which I mention because there isn't going to be a sudden day upon which all conventional cars and all semi-autonomous cars disappear from our roadways. The economics doesn't make this feasible. As such, there will be ongoing chances of human driven cars that will be crashing into or being hit by self-driving driverless cars.

For those various reasons, you cannot carte blanche claim that self-driving driverless cars will eliminate all deaths and injuries resulting from the use of cars.

I suppose far off in the future we might someday in a science fiction kind of way have eventually switched over to self-driving driverless cars and completely done away with human driving, and maybe have some forcefields or flying cars, but that's a Utopian idea and not really a practical way to think about this topic.

Thus, I hope you might agree that instead of using the moral tenet that all fatalities and injuries will be eliminated, instead the more reasonable argument is that some amount of fatalities and injuries will still exist and one hopes or guesses that the number will be less than the count due to today's conventional cars.

We don't yet know though how much less the fatalities and injuries count will be.

As such, this tenet is based on a speculative belief that hopefully there will be less fatalities and injuries, and you can propose mathematical models to try and guess what it might be, but overall no one knows and it could turn out to only be a small dent in the numbers, or one supposes it could actually raise the number of deaths and injuries, depending upon how safe the fully autonomous cars are and how society responds to these systems.

- Eliminate the tedium of driving

A somewhat lower priority item on the list of moral imperatives for achieving self-driving driverless cars involves the suggestion that humans will be relieved of having to do driving and for which driving is labeled as a kind of tedious task.

Yes, one can say that many human drivers find driving to be boring or tedious, and therefore a fully autonomous car by definition does away with that element (since it is the AI doing solo driving).

One counterargument is that some people actually enjoy the driving act. Presumably, true self-driving driverless cars will deny those people the preference or joy of being able to drive (will we tell them they can drive only on closed tracks or special set asides?).

As a society, we have yet to ascertain whether perhaps the good to society of not having human drivers is "fair" for those human drivers that want to be able to drive. It is going to be a thorny topic.

Once again, this moral tenet is not so clearly indisputable.

- Eliminate the stress of driving

I'd wager that almost everyone would agree that driving is stressful, even for those that say they love to drive.

By definition, the stress of driving would no longer exist when the AI is doing the driving solo.

Yet, there's the potential stress of being a passenger inside a self-driving driverless car and hoping that the AI will be able to safely drive the car.

Plus, you the human passenger have little control over the AI driving, other than presumably an ability to speak voice commands to the AI system and request that it drive in some other manner, though the AI might or might not so comply (if you tell the AI to go 10 miles per hour on a freeway, and there's no seeming basis to do so, it likely would be that the AI would not abide by your command).

Some might argue that you are trading the stress of being a driver into the stress of being a rider. You might argue that if that's the case then you already garner stress by getting into a taxi or a ridesharing car as a passenger, though the counterpoint is that doing so involves a human driver at the wheel rather than the AI at the wheel.

Will we eventually reach a point that the passenger in a self-driving driverless car has less stress than if they were in a human driven car? Presumably, but we don't know when or if that will occur.

• Eliminate the logistics of finding a driver

Some would say that the beauty of a self-driving driverless car is that there is always a driver ready to go, the AI system, and thus you don't need to deal with the logistics aspects of finding a driver and getting the driver to come and drive a car.

Yes, this seems pretty airtight.

What we don't yet know is the cost associated with having the always-on always-available AI driver.

Suppose the cost turns out to be higher than using a human driver, including the logistics costs associated with having to find and make use of a human driver.

As a society, are we willing to incur a higher cost for being able to go in a self-driving driverless car, and if so, how much will that be?

I'm not saying the cost will be higher, and it might ultimately be less than the cost of using a human driver, but we just don't yet know which way it will go.

- Provides expanded access to cars for mobility

Another moral imperative voiced is that the advent of self-driving driverless cars will provide expanded access to cars for those that might be mobility marginalized or otherwise not be able to as readily utilize cars today.

Yes, that seems to make sense in that if self-driving driverless cars are roaming around 24x7 and readily available, it would reduce the friction of seeking to be a passenger in a car and leverage that mobility.

Per the earlier point about costs, we don't know what the cost of that added mobility is going to be.

Suppose the cost is so high that it turns out the promised mobility expansion is not viable and therefore self-driving driverless cars are only economically affordable by some. Indeed, there are those that are worried that fully autonomous cars will be used nearly exclusively by the elite and not be available for the rest of us.

Though I personally doubt that kind of scenario emerging, and I do believe that the advent of autonomous cars is going to increase mobility, the point is that we don't know what will happen and thus one cannot make the argument that expanded access will unequivocally occur.

Conclusion

This discussion has tried to indicate that the "moral imperative" is not quite so obvious and nor so indisputable.

Am I then arguing that we should not be pursing self-driving driverless cars?

Heavens no.

I am trying to clarify that when someone tries to wrap themselves into the "moral imperative" cloak, you have to be careful to not become blinded to the reality that we don't yet know how the advent of self-driving driverless cars will turnout.

I say this because there is an ongoing debate about whether or not we should be allowing the emerging autonomous cars, consisting right now of (barely) Level 4 and not yet anywhere near to Level 5, onto our public roadways.

The "moral imperative" clamor can seemingly hide the ugly truth that we don't yet know how safe the existing tryouts are, and nor how long they will need to occur, and nor if these tryouts are actually necessary and sufficient to arrive at true Level 4 and true Level 5.

As I've analyzed in my work (see this article here), it could be that we might incur deaths and injuries now with the emerging Level 4's that would be considered a "trade-off" against the future deaths and injuries if we stick with conventional cars (using Linear Non-Threshold or LNT thinking).

I don't think that society is currently contemplating this as a kind of trade-off and instead tends to assume there won't be any deaths or injuries from the existing public roadway tryouts. Instances such as the Uber pedestrian death in Phoenix last year and the Tesla AutoPilot-related deaths and injuries that some have cited are indicative of how society doesn't seem to be contemplating a deaths and injuries trade-off methodology.

In any case, next time that someone tries to use the "moral imperative" aces card, I trust that you'll be mindful that there is no free lunch and that getting to self-driving driverless cars is a more ambiguous "imperative" and a less clear-cut moral "above all else" doctrine than it might be made out to be (meaning that it eclipses all other concerns or considerations in striving to its aims).

We've seen throughout history the sometimes-untoward aspects that can arise as a result of so-called noble causes crusade.

Just want to add a dose of reality into these pursuits, and meanwhile, yes, I am indeed a proponent of achieving self-driving driverless cars, which I'm working diligently and daily toward that desired goal.

CHAPTER 13

FREED UP DRIVER TIME

AN

AI SELF-DRIVING CAR

CHAPTER 13

FREED UP DRIVER TIME

AN

AI SELF-DRIVING CAR

According to recent analyses, Americans spend about one hour a day driving a car and travel approximately 32 miles in doing so.

Collectively, this amounts to nearly 70 billion hours of driving time annually in the United States alone.

That is 70 billion hours of humans gripping the steering wheel, keeping their eyes on the road (hopefully!), and otherwise undertaking the heady and life-or-death task of driving a car.

Here's a question to consider, namely what will happen to those billions upon billions of driving hours once we have truly self-driving driverless cars available?

Let's unpack the question and see what answer might be revealed.

Advent Of Self-Driving Driverless Cars

I'd like to first establish the difference between fully autonomous cars, ones that the AI drives the car and for which there is no human driver involved (referred to as Level 4 and Level 5 automation), versus the sidekick aspects of semi-autonomous cars that entail the augmentation or system aided support of a human driver (considered Level 2 or Level 3).

For the semi-autonomous cars, the human driver must still be present and alert, since they are expected to be actively immersed in co-sharing of the driving task with the automation.

I realize that you've perhaps seen YouTube videos of drivers that are napping or otherwise not paying attention to the driving task, doing so in a Level 2 or Level 3 car, and all I can say is that this is absolutely (stupidly, recklessly) wrong and absolutely a prescription for dire and untoward consequences.

In theory, the 70 billion hours of annual driving time would still be the same amount of driving time in any Level 2 or Level 3 car.

Sure, you might try to claim that the driving time is possibly not as taxing or arduous because you have the semi-autonomous tech that's helping you drive, but nonetheless you are expected to be mentally and physically ready to drive the car at any moment in time. Thus, I'd assert that it is indeed bona fide driving time and there's no cutting corners in terms of the hours involved.

In the case of truly autonomous cars, the amount of human driving time by definition should drop to zero.

That's because there isn't a human driver in a fully self-driving driverless car. The AI does all of the driving. This suggests that humans will only be passengers and no longer car drivers. Thus, today's car drivers will no longer presumably be drivers and will shift their 70 billion annual hours into becoming passengers.

As an aside, if you are wondering about counting today's passengers in conventional cars, they would still be counted as passengers in self-driving cars, so I don't intend to add their hours of being inside a car into the number of hours of humans being inside self-driving cars. Essentially, I'm suggesting it nets out that if a passenger today is a passenger in a regular car, they will ergo be a passenger in a self-driving car of the future.

Herein I am focused on the change that is coming of human drivers that used to need to be attentive to the driving task and henceforth will no longer need to do so and will transform into becoming passengers.

Will Human Drivers Alter Their In-Car Time

One related matter is whether or not those human drivers will one-for-one switch to passenger hours or perhaps they might opt to spend either less hours or possibly more hours inside a car.

Here's the logic.

A human driver today might be making some number of trips to cart around somebody else. For example, suppose you drive your kids to school each day. If that's the case, and if a self-driving car can take your kids to school for you, there's no need for you to go along. In that case, you aren't going to swap that particular driving time into doing the same act as before, not even as a passenger.

You could then argue that the 70 billion hours of annual driving time might not directly become 70 billion hours of passenger time, and instead it might drop by a little or maybe a lot. Could it translate into 50 billion hours or maybe 30 billion hours?

Could be, but nobody knows as yet.

Alternatively, those human drivers might end-up increasing the time they spend inside a car.

Let's pretend that you work in a downtown area and purposely live relatively close to downtown to keep your commute minimized, partially because you hate to drive. After self-driving cars become prevalent, you decide that you'd prefer to live out in the countryside, which will be easy to do since the AI system is going to deal with the driving act for you. You can nap in the driverless car during the commute.

If that kind of behavior arises, the 70 billion hours of driving time might leap upward in terms of being translated into passenger time. Maybe those drivers will take all kinds of longer trips or more frequent trips because they are relieved of the driving task.

Could it become 80 billion or even 100 billion hours converted into passenger time?

Yes, possibly, but nobody knows.

How To Use That Time

I'll make the rather reasonable assumption that by-and-large the 70 billion hours of annual driving time is going to become passenger time, plus or minus some number of billions, if you will.

What in the heck are people going to do with this newly found time?

One thing you can say for sure, this portends a humungous marketing opportunity for companies wanting to advertise their products and services.

Think about those millions of Americans now comfortably ensconced in their driverless cars, able to be attentive to your ad or marketing campaign, and it makes marketers mouths water.

Those former drivers are now freed from thinking about the driving task. Time for you to fill those minds with ads. A bonanza!

Well, besides our becoming likely inundated with marketing messages and bombarded with ads, what else might we do while now becoming a passenger inside a self-driving driverless car.

Here's some ideas:

Sleep. As mentioned, people might move further away from work and therefore catch a snooze while heading to the office or heading home from the office. The interior of self-driving cars is predicted to accommodate the desire to take naps, including fully reclining seats and special darkened shades for the windows. Whether you will feel safe enough to fall asleep in a driverless car is another matter altogether.

Do work. You might work while inside your self-driving car, using the Internet and your in-car laptop or computer, along with being able to do remote Skype-like sessions with other workers that are in the office or similarly commuting in other self-driving cars. We don't yet know whether this will be working time that gets lopped off your normal 8 hours a day of work, or it might merely get piled on top of your workday and now you'll be expected to work more hours than you did while driving.

Stare out the window. As a driver, you had to concentrate on the roadway and other traffic. Shifting to becoming a passenger, you can comfortably scan the surroundings and let your eyes wander leisurely. This could be a boon for billboards and cars with exterior displayed ads, though it might be that people decide they don't care to look outside and instead focus their attention inside the self-driving car.

Play online games. You could play games on your smartphone. There will likely be sizable LED displays inside the self-driving car and thus you can use those to play games. Maybe you'll wear a Virtual Reality (VR) headset and play games immersed in your own world while zooming along a driverless car. To get you to look outside the car, there are bound to be Augmented Reality (AR) games too, either requiring you to wear special goggles or perhaps the windows of the self-driving car will be made to do the same.

Interact with fellow humans in the car. You might use the time inside a self-driving car to interact with fellow humans. It is assumed that driverless cars will likely have swivel seats, allowing several people in the car to swivel and face each other. Perhaps you'll commute to work with fellow workers and carryon work discussions, or maybe you'll party like its 1999.

Get training or a degree. You'll have online access and sizable LED displays so you could try to get some added training or even do your college degree while cruising around in your self-driving car. The educational sessions might be based on video or it could be undertaken live. There you are, waving your hands at your fellow students, all spread around the country and inside their self-driving cars too.

Watch cat videos. I'm being a bit flippant, but you could watch tons of cat videos while inside your self-driving car. Actually, my point is that there is the opportunity for an entertainment explosion of content needed to satisfy the mental hunger of those humans shifting their 70 billion hours into sitting inside a self-driving car. Entertainment galore!

Perform private acts. I won't say much about this topic, other than noting that for those that seemed to relish the mile-high club, they will now be able to add to their scorecard the 65 mile per hour club. Since there's no human driver, there's no witness and no space taken up for a driver. Enough said.

Undertake a hobby. With the freeing up of the interior space of a car due to the removal of a driver's seat, there are all sorts of ways to reconfigure things. Maybe you like to cook and will use the inside of the car as a mini kitchen to prepare your lunch for the day. If you like plants, perhaps you have several potted plants that you provide tender care too while on a driving journey. Endless possibilities.

Become bored or have Zen time. For completeness sake, I suppose you could be in the driverless car and do nothing or the seeming equivalent of it. Does being bored count as a form of entertainment? Does using the time for Zen count as educational?

Be scared, very scared. Presumably, you won't be willing to be a passenger inside a self-driving car unless you believe it is safe to do so. Of course, even if it is safe, you might anyway still harbor concerns. As such, you might become otherwise frozen or immobilized in the sense that you are unable to do anything during the driving journey other than hope and pray that the driverless car provides you with a safe ride.

Conclusion

What will you do with the shift of your driving time of today to becoming instead passenger time in a self-driving driverless car of the future?

Some say this is the same as though you opted to give up your car and started taking the bus or subway or a train.

I disagree.

When you take a bus or any similar kind of public transportation, you lose the privacy bubble that you had while inside a car. You cannot as readily do the same things on a public transport as you can in the (usually) less public confines of a car.

Furthermore, on public transport you cannot cart around much with you, other than perhaps a backpack or purse. In the case of being inside a self-driving car, it could be outfitted with a small kitchen as mentioned earlier or have your stamp collection or your toy boat making equipment, etc.

Now I'm not suggesting that self-driving cars won't be used as a form of public transport. I'm sure they will. They though also offer a kind of private compartment that is not readily duplicated in traditional mass transit.

In any case, if I've left out something that you have in mind to do while inside a self-driving driverless car, my kudos to you for identifying other things to do.

There are also likely paths to great wealth for those that find something for people to do in their self-driving cars and that you could sell to people that particular thing or activity.

Suppose you could somehow get people to spend a measly one dollar toward you, doing so for each of the 70 billion hours of shifted driving time into passenger time, you'd be rolling in dough due to the advent of true self-driving driverless cars.

Start thinking about it.

CHAPTER 14

DEADLIEST HIGHWAYS

AND

AI SELF-DRIVING CARS

CHAPTER 14

DEADLIEST HIGHWAYS
AND
AI SELF-DRIVING CARS

If you are heading on a driving trip this summer, please avoid the following highways:

- I-5 in California

- US-1 in Florida

- I-10 in Texas

- I-75 in Georgia

- I-10 in Arizona

Those are considered the top five deadliest summertime highways, according to a recent analysis of National Highway Traffic Safety Administration (NHTSA) data on highway fatalities in the United States.

The rankings of the highways were based on the number of human fatalities due to car accidents in the May through September timeframe, covering the years of 2015 to 2017 (the most recently available data).

Deadliest Highways Explained

Why are those particular highways so deadly?

The most likely explanation is because they are generally the main arteries for travel in those respective states and therefore, especially during the summer, a lot of traffic translates into a lot of car accidents, which then translates into (sadly) fatalities.

It could be that many of the drivers are unfamiliar with those highways and have come to the area as tourists, often confused about which offramp to take or how they should properly drive as per local customs.

Maybe the regular drivers get fed up with the touristy drivers and when you mix the two together, it becomes a potent and explosive combination. Get out of my darned way, says the seasoned local driver, and meanwhile the driver from out-of-town is upset that the other drivers aren't allowing them to dart into and out of traffic, doing so because they are lost and unsure of where to go.

These deadliest highways themselves don't seem to be in disrepair, which could be another reason for a high frequency of accidents. You might argue that the signage is at times lacking or confusing, but that's not bound to be a significant factor in the fatalities count.

It could be that drivers on those highways are driving at high speeds.

Setting aside whether the driver is a local or out-of-towner, pretty much everyone in a car on those highways is going to be driving fast. Since the highways are a main artery, it also tends to include slower and lumbering trucks and cargo vehicles, moving along at the (nearly glacial) speed limit, and creating a dramatic disparity in speed between the tortoises and the hares.

I'm not going to get bogged down in the ongoing debates about speed limits on open highways, which is a continual argumentative fight that recurs in our society. Some say that if we lowered the speed limits it would save lives, or if the chances of getting a ticket for speeding was heightened it would save lives.

Others refute that the high speed is the "cause" of the fatalities. Yes, there is usually a correlation between speed and traffic fatalities, but it can be argued that it is misleading to claim that there is a direct causation between the speed and fatalities.

In any case, if you believe that the highway itself is not prompting the fatalities, and even if speed is involved, presumably the buck-stops-here must be the drivers.

It's those drivers that are at the root of the fatalities.

Magically, if today's drivers could somehow be transformed into becoming better drivers, being always alert and on top of their game, those enhanced drivers would presumably deal adroitly with higher speeds (if that is the issue), and therefore in a more perfect world those upgraded drivers would reduce or eliminate the production of fatalities.

Well, it's plainly the case that getting human drivers to become better at driving is not an easy assignment. Humans tend to resist change. They tend to get bored or distracted while driving. They get upset and allow their emotions to carry over into their driving decisions. And so on.

Okay, if we can't change humans to be better drivers, perhaps we ought to replace them.

As such, once we have true self-driving driverless cars, ones being driven entirely by AI and there is no human driver involved, what might happen on those deadliest summertime highways?

Let's unpack the question and see what we can discover.

Advent Of Self-Driving Cars

I'd like to clarify that there is a distinction between fully autonomous self-driving driverless cars, known as Level 4 and Level 5, and cars that are semi-autonomous involving the co-sharing of the driving task with a human driver (referred to as Level 2 and Level 3).

You could try to argue that the semi-autonomous cars will increasingly provide automation that will aid human drivers in becoming better at driving. As such, perhaps the added automation is going to reduce those deadliest highways fatalities.

It might, but it is hard to say whether this will be true.

Keep in mind that you still have the same human driver in-the-loop as you did when the automation was less capable. One concern is that drivers will become complacent, discounting their role as a co-shared driver, and end-up getting into car accidents that they would otherwise have not gotten into, simply due to mentally drifting from the driving task under the false belief that the automation would save them (which it might not).

I'm not going to tackle herein the matter of how semi-autonomous cars are going to impact our deadliest highways situation and instead focus on the true self-driving driverless cars (which we don't yet have, and for which we barely have Level 4's, a constrained version of full autonomy, doing limited public roadway tryouts).

Most pundits would likely declare that once we have true driverless cars it will so radically change our world that the number of fatalities on our deadliest highways would drop to zero.

Those same pundits would even go further and be willing to state that the number of fatalities on all and any highways will become zero.

Essentially, no deadliest highways anymore.

All highways become undeadly.

All highways will have zero fatalities.

Though it would be heartening and uplifting to go along with the zero fatalities notion, it is an overly simplistic viewpoint and (unfortunately) not going to happen.

There are several bona fide reasons that we are still going to have fatalities on our highways and streets.

First, on streets there will be pedestrians and those pedestrians can take sudden and unexpected actions that belie the physics of any car, whether human driven or AI driven, being able to stop in time to prevent either a fatality or an injury.

You might say that pedestrians won't be on highways, and though generally true, there is still a chance of pedestrians getting mixed into highways, though admittedly slim. There are though motorcyclists, which if humans are still allowed to ride motorcycles, provides a possibility of having true driverless cars getting into accidents due to motorcycle entanglement that could lead to fatalities or injuries.

Furthermore, the idea that we are going to overnight switch out conventional cars and suddenly have only driverless cars is a silly and obviously untenable possibility.

The economics won't allow this to occur.

Therefore, there will be a mixture of driverless cars and human driven cars on our highways.

Some say that we ought to restrict human driven cars once there is a prevalence of self-driving cars, perhaps setting aside designated lanes that are only for driverless cars, or only for human driven cars. Another idea is that human driven cars might be restricted to being used only at certain times of the day or certain days of the week. Will human drivers put up with such restrictions?

An additional factor that many aren't considering is the chances of the AI having any latent bugs or errors in it. Plus, the specialized sensors and computer processors can have faults or failures. And, a car is still a car, meaning that the kinds of car issues that can arise will still occur, including blown out tires and other physical breakdowns.

All in all, we don't yet know how this will playout.

It seems pretty certain that we will have a mixture of human driven cars and driverless cars, along with human driven motorcycles and pedestrians, which will continue for the foreseeable future.

As an aside, there are efforts to turn motorcycles into semi-autonomous and even fully autonomous versions (see my article here about these advances).

Figuring Out The Fatalities Hotspots

My point about the advent of driverless cars is that we will continue to have fatalities, though one would hope it will be less than the number that we incur today.

Suppose the real-world impact of the driverless cars is that we do indeed have less fatalities, oddly enough it could be that those deadliest highways would still be the deadliest highways.

Allow me to explain.

Perhaps the mixture of driverless cars and human driven cars on those particular highways will continue to have fatalities. If the number of such fatalities is lessened, it would imply those highways are now "safer" as a presumed result of having the driverless cars. That's good.

Meanwhile, suppose we make the assumption that all other highways are also being lessened in terms of the number of fatalities, once again due to the driverless cars entering into the picture. That's good too.

Yet, it could be that those specific deadliest highways will still have the highest number of fatalities, in comparison to other highways, albeit at a lesser count than the highways usage of today involving conventional cars.

Ergo, those deadliest highways are still the deadliest ones.

There's another possible twist.

Maybe the fatality counts on the existing deadliest highways drops precipitously. That's good.

Suppose though that the other highways aren't being frequented by self-driving cars as much. It could be that with a limited supply of driverless cars that those scarce and costly vehicles will be positioned in locales where they can make the most money, likely the places where those existing deadliest highways are.

This could then mean that those other highways will now become likelier candidates for being the deadliest highways.

Another qualm some have expressed is that human drivers might gradually find themselves becoming deskilled in the driving task.

Why?

Well, if you are routinely using a fully autonomous car, you aren't exercising your driving abilities.

You might stop driving for a while and your driving skills begin to decay, meanwhile for your summer vacation you decide to rent a car, a conventional car or even a semi-autonomous car, and now all of a sudden you are behind the wheel again.

This might increase the chances of car fatalities when you have large segments of society that nearly gave up driving and then opt to jump back into the driver's seat.

Conclusion

It is conceivable that instead of open highways being the deadliest roadways, perhaps the deadliest driving locales would shift toward the outskirts of cities.

Here's the logic.

On the open roads, let's suppose that the driverless cars help in reducing the traffic fatalities. Pretend also that those long stretches would be driven primarily by truly autonomous cars and trucks.

Back towards town, we might have a larger mixture of human driven cars and autonomous vehicles, along with the plethora of pedestrians, bicyclists, and motorcyclists. Inside the core part of a city or town, the speeds would be low enough that car accidents involving driverless cars or conventional cars would produce injuries but hopefully not as many fatalities.

The speeds at the outskirts of a city might be higher, such as on local freeways, tending toward more severe impacts when car accidents occur, producing fatalities.

Some number of years from now, once we have a prevalence of self-driving driverless cars, the deadliest roadways might be the freeways bordering and interconnecting cities. An added basis for thinking this would be that some assert that with the emergence of self-driving cars that people will decide to live further outside of the cities, commuting to work via the ease of using a driverless car.

The volume of car traffic at the outskirts of cities might correspondingly increase as a result of that societal shift in where people live and work.

Anyway, please drive safely this summer and if you aren't able to avoid the deadliest highways, I ask that you keep your eyes open and your mind focused on driving your car. You, your family, and the lives of others that might be on their summertime vacation could depend on it.

CHAPTER 15

YOUR LYIN' EYES

AND

AI SELF-DRIVING CARS

CHAPTER 15

YOUR LYIN' EYES

AND

AI SELF-DRIVING CARS

You might be somewhat familiar with the expression "lyin' eyes" and which can be used in a variety of interesting and useful ways.

Especially popularized by a famous song that the Eagles brought to the world in the mid-70's, the most straightforward meaning of lying eyes is that your eyes have the potential of giving away your true intent, in spite of your actions that might suggest some other purpose or goal.

Lore has it that Don Henley and Glenn Frey of the Eagles were inspired to incorporate the expression as the title of their song in order to describe how some beautiful women were cheating on their husbands and that apparently those cheating women's lyin' eyes gave away their unfaithful efforts.

There are though other variations to the meaning of lying eyes.

Another interpretation for the notion of lyin' eyes is that sometimes your eyes see one thing, but what you thought you saw is not what was actually there.

That's a mouthful, so let me elaborate.

The other day I was walking in downtown San Francisco and I caught a glimpse of someone on the crowded sidewalk that looked just like a college chum of mine that I haven't seen for many years. I did one of those double takes whereby you look, you become momentarily startled, and you look again, staring intently to figure out whether what you thought you saw was true.

I even tried to hurriedly catch-up with the person but gave up when I realized upon further visual inspection that it wasn't my friend from long ago.

Did my eyes lie to me?

Maybe, though one has to also add the brain into the equation of what you see versus what you think that you see.

In many ways, your eyes are relatively simplistic in terms of mainly serving as a sensory device to capture images, and those images are then relayed to the brain to figure out what the images might mean. You could suggest that the eyes are like a camera, taking a picture and the image has no particular meaning until the mind works its magic by analyzing what was visually captured.

A twist on this version of lyin' eyes is that you can potentially convince yourself that you saw something that wasn't there at all.

Witnesses called into courtroom are notorious for oftentimes misremembering things that they believe they saw. Yes, your honor, the man was carrying a gun, I'm sure of it, someone might testify.

Shockingly, suppose that it was later proven via say a video recording that the accused was not carrying a gun.

Why did the witness so confidently and assuredly believe that the person had a gun?

Assuming that the witness is being sincere, it is quite feasible that the witness during the in-the-moment effort had in their mind that the person was threatening looking, which could have invoked a context in their mind encompassing the realm of weapons as part of the dangerous moment, ultimately causing their mind to enact or imagine a weapon into the scene, though it wasn't really there.

As you can plainly now see, lyin' eyes is a handy expression that offers plenty of options for its usage.

Here's an interesting facet to consider: While riding in a true self-driving car, what if you see something occurring in traffic that is not in alignment with what the driverless car is "seeing" or that the driverless car is seemingly not reacting to?

Which should you then believe, the self-driving car or perhaps what might be your lyin' eyes?

Let's unpack this question and consider the ramifications of the matter.

Human Lyin' Eyes And Semi-Autonomous Cars

Before we can closely examine the question, it is important to clarify that I am going to primarily concentrate on fully autonomous cars, often considered at a Level 4 or Level 5.

A true self-driving driverless car is one that the AI is completely driving the car and there is no human driving involved.

In contrast, a Level 2 or Level 3 car is known as a semi-autonomous car, meaning that there must be a human driver present and that the automation and the human driver are co-sharing the driving task.

During the emergence of Level 3 cars, there is admittedly a possibility of having lyin' eyes issues.

You and the automation are co-sharing the driving task in a Level 3 car, which provokes a dangerous gambit that the automation might try to do one thing, while your eyes and your mind believe that something else should be undertaken.

Similarly, you might be trying to take a particular action with the driving controls, and yet the automation might "disagree" and try to assert that you should be doing something else instead.

We have yet to universally figure out the balance between when the automation wins out versus when the co-sharing driving human wins out. You might be tempted to claim that the human should always win out, especially since they are considered the legally responsible driving party, but this is not such an easy and always appropriate answer.

Consider a situation whereby a Level 3 car is about to crash into a truck that's come to a halt in front of the Level 3 car, and suppose the human driver is pushing on the gas pedal because they haven't yet realized the aspect that they are about crash head-on into the truck.

Should the automation invoke the brakes of the car?

Well, of course it should, you would say, but notice that at this juncture of the scenario that the human driving action is completely contrary to the action that the automation is seeking to undertake.

The human is accelerating, yet the automation wants to hit the brakes. I've setup the situation so that it would seem obvious that the human is "wrong" and the automation is "right" in this use case, but I can readily provide other scenarios that are just the opposite.

I hope you can now realize why it is difficult to carte blanche pre-determine whether the human wins or the automation wins when they are at cross-purposes of each other (I can provide you with numerous other such indeterminable examples).

Semi-autonomous cars are opening a can of worms due to the co-sharing actions of a human driver and an automation form of driver, thus forcing that the two "drivers" to jointly collaborate during the driving act, a real-time life-or-death act that at-times is going to (sadly) be an untenable collaboration.

Let's shift now to focus on the lyin' eyes when you are inside a fully autonomous self-driving car.

Human Lyin' Eyes And Fully Autonomous Cars

It's a nice sunny day.

You are enjoying riding in your fancy new self-driving car.

What a wonderful world we live in that you no longer need to take the wheel of the car, and nor do you need to listen to a tiresome human driver that would be driving the car if you were getting a ridesharing lift in a conventional car.

As the driverless car makes its way down the street of your neighborhood, you are looking out the windows of the car, noticing the other homes on your block and the magnificent trees that look so majestic and offer cool shade on this hot and muggy summertime day.

All of a sudden, a ball bounces out into the street.

You look furtively to see if little Joey or little Samantha are maybe playing in their front yard and have inadvertently let their ball go past themselves and into roadway.

Us humans know the age-old logic that where there's a bouncing ball there is a good chance that a child will soon be running out into the street to try and get the wayward ball.

Here's the rub.

Does the AI of the self-driving car also "know" that a bouncing ball implies a soon to be appearing child into the roadway and possibly into the path of the oncoming car?

Maybe yes, maybe no.

It could be that the AI has simply detected the ball as an object that perchance is now in the street.

Upon detecting the ball, the AI might determine that the ball is small enough to not pose a threat to the car.

The AI might opt to continue straight ahead, maybe doing so because a mathematical calculation has indicated that the ball won't hit the car on its current path, thus, there's no special action needed by the self-driving car.

Or, maybe the AI opts to slightly swerve the car to avoid hitting the ball, if it seems that mathematically the path of the ball and the heretofore path of the driverless car are going to intersect. The swerve is calculated as feasible since there is nothing else in the street at this moment in time that would get hit by the change in the path of the self-driving car.

This all could occur without the AI in any manner whatsoever doing any kind of prediction about what the ball means and what might happen next. Instead, the AI might be programmed to deal with whatever happens to happen at whatever moment it happens, lacking any predictive feature to anticipate what might happen in the near future.

You've perhaps seen novice teenage drivers do the same thing, namely, they act upon whatever they see in real-time and fail to consider the future ramifications of a driving scene that is unfolding or stepwise revealing itself.

Meanwhile, what about you, the human passenger inside the driverless car.

You are now personally alert to the possibility that at any moment a child might dart into the street, but you have no idea whether the AI is considering the same possibility.

If the driverless car continues straight ahead and does not change its course, you might assume that the AI hasn't figured out that a child could be soon in the path of the car.

On the other hand, if the self-driving car does a slight swerving, you won't know whether the swerving action is merely to avoid hitting the ball, or whether it might be an anticipatory move to be ready in case a child does run into the street.

All in all, should you believe your lyin' eyes, which are telling you that a ball is in the street and might be a precursor to a child suddenly running into the street (an idea that's in your mind, at that juncture), or should you merely assume and hope and pray that the AI is ready for the chance of a child darting in front of the self-driving car?

Your peaceful ride in the self-driving car has just transformed into one of grave concern and anxiousness.

What should you do?

Dealing With Your Lyin' Eyes

So far, we have a ball loose in the street, for which your eyes see the ball and let's assume there is no disputing the fact that there is a ball there in the roadway.

In your mind's eye, you also envision a child soon to follow that ball. The speed of the driverless car and its ongoing direction are going to make for a rather sour outcome if a child does dart into the street.

I realize that some AI developers would say that the AI would be scanning the side of the road to detect whether there is a child nearby. Yes, that could be possible, but let's assume that there are those majestic trees blocking the view of the area where a child might be, and thus the AI cannot readily spot any children.

You as a passenger have no driving controls. You are completely dependent upon whatever the AI decides to do about the driving of the self-driving car.

Presumably, you could try to ask the AI whether it is going to get ready in case a child darts into the street, which is the kind of conversation or dialogue that you might have with a human driver in a conventional car, wherein you might have deduced the chances of a child appearing and want to make sure that the human driver is thinking the same thing.

Well, even though self-driving cars are going to have Natural Language Processing (NLP) capabilities, akin to the likes of Alexa and Siri, it is unknown as yet as to how sophisticated the AI NLP will be.

Early versions of self-driving cars might have quite simplistic AI NLP and therefore your attempt to discuss or dialogue with the driverless car won't be viable.

Even if you could converse with the AI, what should the AI do about whatever you might say regarding the driving task?

In this use case about the ball, I realize it seems obvious that if you alert the AI that presumably the AI should follow your instructions and get ready for a child darting into the street. On the other hand, suppose you are drunk and tell the self-driving car to go toward the curb, making things even worse if a child does come out into the street.

A human driver would have overall common sense and be able to figure out the nuances of a myriad of situations, while the AI system is unlikely to be able to do so. Indeed, please be aware that there is not as yet anything close to any kind of common-sense reasoning capability for AI systems.

I know that some AI developers will carp that I'm implying that human drivers are failproof and will always do the right thing, which is not at all what I am saying.

What I am saying is that the AI systems are going to be a far cry from being a human driver, which means that in many respects maybe the AI will do a better job (presumably not get drunk, not get distracted, etc.), and in many other respects, a whole lot of respects, the AI will be a many times less capable than what a human driver can do (at least for now and the foreseeable future).

Conclusion

There are going to be situations of humans riding in a self-driving car that involve the humans having lyin' eyes of seeing something that they believe is happening, or might happen, and for which the human rider won't know whether the AI is "thinking" the same things or not.

Some might argue that this is easily solved by having the AI continually report to the rider about the driving scene.

I doubt doing so is much of a solution.

Riders might get inundated by this kind of continual reporting, eventually either ignoring it or becoming numb to it.

Also, suppose a child is alone in the self-driving car, what good is it to be telling a young child about the driving actions.

Furthermore, even if an adult passenger is staying on the edge of their seat to act as a kind of imaginary backseat driver, keep in mind that the human passenger won't have driving controls, therefore whatever they might want the car to do will only be done by trying to convince the AI to take such an action.

Anyway, when you get into a true self-driving car, don't be surprised if you hear the song Lyin' Eyes playing on the radio, which might be a singularity trick by the AI to subliminally convince you to not believe your eyes and instead believe the "eyes" (cameras) of the AI system.

Whether you should you try to hide your lying eyes from the inward facing camera of the AI system, you'll need to decide.

CHAPTER 16

ELON MUSK

PHYSICS MINDSET

AND

AI SELF-DRIVING CARS

CHAPTER 16

ELON MUSK PHYSICS MINDSET
AND
AI SELF-DRIVING CARS

Leaders often use specific mental models to guide their approach to leadership.

Allow me to provide an example.

I was brought into an up-and-coming high-tech firm to do some management consulting work due to a recent organizational change that had been made.

The board of directors had earlier decided to replace the CEO with someone that they had recruited straight out of the military.

As a senior officer and having had a lengthy successful career in the army, the new CEO proceeded to try and run the company in a military-like way. This was quite counter to the culture of the firm and ultimately caused quite a number of difficulties and issues.

Had the new CEO leveraged his military background and been willing to adapt it to the commercial sector, the result might have been different and possibly been a boost to the high-tech company. Instead, he got bogged down in what he already knew, serving as a kind of mental anchor, shaping all of his actions as the top leader of the firm.

In that sense, a mental model that guides leadership behavior can be a dual-edged sword.

On the one hand, the mental model provides a handy framework for being able to make decisions and take executive actions, doing so with the belief that if it has worked well before and therefore it will certainly work well again.

Unfortunately, it can also be a subtle and sometimes unrealized trap, causing the leader to see the world through the lens of the mental model even when the model might be misapplied or misappropriated to a new situation.

Shifting to another example, consider the case of Tesla and what's taking place there.

Elon Musk is a leader that has oftentimes touted the importance of physics to his way of thinking and how and why he has taken various actions, repeatedly mentioning and explaining his behavior by using physics as a predominant mental model for much of what he does.

You can readily find published quotes of his such as "physics is a good framework for thinking" and "I tend to approach things from a physics framework," which dovetails into one of his bachelor's degrees being in physics and his initial pursuit of a Ph.D. in physics (he left after two days, opting to pursue other opportunities).

Let's consider how this physics mindset has and continues to shape his leadership efforts.

And, in particular, consider too that perhaps his physics mindset might be stoking his hopes and views on soon achieving full self-driving cars at Tesla, of which few in the self-driving car industry believe is likely and express qualms about a stated overreach in a moonshot-like achievement.

Status Of Tesla Toward True Self-Driving Cars

There is a myriad of speculative reasons being given as to why Elon Musk believes so fervently that Tesla is on the cusp of presumably achieving true self-driving cars.

As clarification, most would agree that a true self-driving car is one that can operate fully autonomously, meaning that the AI is driving the car and there is no human driving involved at all, often referred to as a Level 4 or Level 5 on the autonomous car scale.

The Level 2, which is generally the classification for the current Tesla models, even when including today's AutoPilot, and the Level 3, which is gradually emerging, consist of semi-autonomous capabilities that require a human driver be at the wheel of the car.

Any such co-sharing arrangement requiring a human driver and AI is not properly classified as being autonomous or fully autonomous, and instead is at best semi-autonomous.

According to numerous comments made by Elon Musk, there is an implication that Tesla is on the verge of having a truly autonomous or fully autonomous self-driving capability soon, perhaps by the end of this year or sometime into the first part of next year.

Many have tried to parse his words to figure out if that's what he is indicating since there is ambiguity in how he has expressed the matter. There are numerous heated and acrimonious debates about what he has stated in his actual words versus what those words imply.

Assuming for the moment that indeed the implication is that fully autonomous car capability is within the grasp of Tesla, it would be a rather remarkable and unexpected miraculous turn of events if that was actually true.

There has been sparse publicly presented evidentiary indication by Tesla that they are really so close to achieving true self-driving cars, and the Autonomy Investor Day event in April did little to shore-up such a promise (it was merely Machine Learning 101 kinds of presentations).

Why then does it seem that Elon Musk believes Tesla is nearing true self-driving car realization, perhaps these reasons might apply:

• Because he knows it to be true and indeed it is going to happen as he has predicted it will,

• Because he wants it to happen, though there might be a gap between what he wants and what the firm is actually going to be able to achieve,

• Because he is using marketing parlance to gain attention to Tesla in the desire to sell more Tesla cars and keep the company underway,

• Because as a strident entrepreneur he has beat the odds before and in this case though the odds might be steep he is using the belief as a motivator for Tesla to strive mightily,

• Because his physics mindset is spurring him to underestimate the difficulty of achieving true self-driving cars and causing him to equate the AI of self-driving car to being akin to any other kind of thorny physics problem.

You are welcome to choose any of the aforementioned reasons, and you might even have some additional reasons that come to your mind.

For now, herein let's take a closer look at the point about his perhaps overreliance on a physics mindset.

Time to unpack it.

Physics As A Mental Model

Physics is great.

I wanted to start with that declarative statement so that you'll know that I am not somehow going to argue that physics is sour or untoward.

Not only is physics great, it has pretty much done well for Elon Musk.

Want to do space travel?

If so, physics is a key underpinning. Musk has had rather remarkable success in the realm of space travel.

Want to bore big tunnels underground?

If so, physics is a key foundational aspect. Musk has had some success in the realm of boring tunnels.

Want to capture and harness solar energy?

If so, physics is a vital aspect. Musk has had modest success in the realm of solar energy.

Want to make a car that uses batteries and is an exciting EV?

If so, physics counts.

For Tesla, there is no denying that their cars are a wonderment of physics and the achievement of EV into the everyday world.

Overall, the theme is that physics has been a boon for Elon Musk in terms of the endeavors that he has pursued.

As such, the physics mental model has become increasingly strengthen. With each success, the outright virtue of deploying a physics approach gets further and further reinforced.

This takes us to the rub.

The rub is that the AI to achieve a true self-driving car is not seemingly a physics problem per se.

Unfortunately, if that's indeed the case, a staunch belief in physics is going to go awry and try to bat away at solving a problem that sits outside the mental model being used.

The mental model could lead to understating the problem and overinflating the ways or chances or speed at solving the problem.

AI Of Self-Driving Cars Is Not Physics Per Se

What does it mean to suggest that the AI for self-driving cars is not a physics problem?

Currently, nobody really knows how the brain works.

Some would assert that the AI needed to drive a car has to be "equivalent" to human thinking in the sense that the AI has to be able to do the same kind of mental processing that human drivers do. This does not necessarily mean that the human brain has to be recreated into a machine, as it could also be that we are somehow able to simulate how the brain works and achieve the same end-result of being able to "think" in a relevant manner.

Suppose you believe that the brain is a physics problem.

You would possibly be searching to find the equations such as Einstein's "e equals mc squared" kind of postulation that would universally explain how the brain functions.

You would get the best "physicists" of the brain to crack it and figure out how the darned thing works.

The reality is that today we are a far cry from being anywhere close to discovering the formulas that reveal the inner processing of the human brain. No matter how many scientists and engineers you throw at the problem, we just aren't there yet.

Therefore, if you envision that achieving true autonomous cars requires being able to solve the problem of how the human brain functions, which could be claimed as essential to putting into AI the driving capability of a human driver, you've got to assuage yourself to a long journey ahead.

This is also partially why achieving Level 3 cars is somewhat easier, since you are still reliant upon having a human driver at the wheel, being able to takeover when the automation cannot handle a driving situation. Thus, a Level 3 that maybe can stretch to say 90% of what a human driver can do (this does not yet exist), would still need that human driver in the driver's seat to provide the remaining 10%.

For a truly autonomous car, the AI must be able to do 100% of what a human driver could do.

It's a tall order.

Now, I am not saying that the human brain defies the laws of physics. Of course, it does not. There is no question that the brain is a physical composition and abides by the physics of our times.

Yet, let's be clear, physics has not been able to explain the mysteries of how the mass of brain in our skulls arises to being able to think. Chemistry doesn't explain it either. Engineering doesn't explain it.

Neuroscience is trying to explain it, but we are still only at the primitives of discovery.

Many researchers in many domains are all tackling the enduring secrets of how minds emerge from the matter of our brains.

Conclusion

Some would suggest that Elon Musk's efforts to reorganize the Tesla AutoPilot team is an indicator of the physics mindset, namely attempting to reshape and replant the best "physicists" (AI developers) in the belief that doing so will solve the human driving AI problem.

Could his rock-solid physics foundation be leading him down a primrose path on solving the AI self-driving car capability problem?

As mentioned earlier, a mental model of a leader can be a dual-edged sword.

It's like the famous indication that if you have a hammer in-hand then everything appears to be a nail.

A physics mindset might do well in lots of circumstances, but when it hits a problem that does not seem especially suited to a physics framework, a leader can find themselves trying to use a hammer when the hammer isn't going to get the results they desire.

We'll have to wait and see what transpires.

APPENDIX

APPENDIX A
TEACHING WITH THIS MATERIAL

The material in this book can be readily used either as a supplemental to other content for a class, or it can also be used as a core set of textbook material for a specialized class. Classes where this material is most likely used include any classes at the college or university level that want to augment the class by offering thought provoking and educational essays about AI and self-driving cars.

In particular, here are some aspects for class use:

o   Computer Science. Studying AI, autonomous vehicles, etc.

o   Business. Exploring technology and it adoption for business.

o   Sociology. Sociological views on the adoption and advancement of technology.

Specialized classes at the undergraduate and graduate level can also make use of this material.

For each chapter, consider whether you think the chapter provides material relevant to your course topic. There is plenty of opportunity to get the students thinking about the topic and force them to decide whether they agree or disagree with the points offered and positions taken. I would also encourage you to have the students do additional research beyond the chapter material presented (I provide next some suggested assignments they can do).

RESEARCH ASSIGNMENTS ON THESE TOPICS

Your students can find background material on these topics, doing so in various business and technical publications. I list below the top ranked AI related journals. For business publications, I would suggest the usual culprits such as the Harvard Business Review, Forbes, Fortune, WSJ, and the like.

Here are some suggestions of homework or projects that you could assign to students:

a) <u>Assignment for foundational AI research topic</u>: Research and prepare a paper and a presentation on a specific aspect of Deep AI, Machine Learning, ANN, etc. The paper should cite at least 3 reputable sources. Compare and contrast to what has been stated in this book.

b) <u>Assignment for the Self-Driving Car topic</u>: Research and prepare a paper and Self-Driving Cars. Cite at least 3 reputable sources and analyze the characterizations. Compare and contrast to what has been stated in this book.

c) <u>Assignment for a Business topic</u>: Research and prepare a paper and a presentation on businesses and advanced technology. What is hot, and what is not? Cite at least 3 reputable sources. Compare and contrast to the depictions in this book.

d) <u>Assignment to do a Startup:</u> Have the students prepare a paper about how they might startup a business in this realm. They must submit a sound Business Plan for the startup. They could also be asked to present their Business Plan and so should also have a presentation deck to coincide with it.

You can certainly adjust the aforementioned assignments to fit to your particular needs and the class structure. You'll notice that I ask for 3 reputable cited sources for the paper writing based assignments. I usually steer students toward "reputable" publications, since otherwise they will cite some oddball source that has no credentials other than that they happened to write something and post it onto the Internet. You can define "reputable" in whatever way you prefer, for example some faculty think Wikipedia is not reputable while others believe it is reputable and allow students to cite it.

The reason that I usually ask for at least 3 citations is that if the student only does one or two citations they usually settle on whatever they happened to find the fastest. By requiring three citations, it usually seems to force them to look around, explore, and end-up probably finding five or more, and then whittling it down to 3 that they will actually use.

I have not specified the length of their papers, and leave that to you to tell the students what you prefer. For each of those assignments, you could end-up with a short one to two pager, or you could do a dissertation length paper. Base the length on whatever best fits for your class, and the credit amount of the assignment within the context of the other grading metrics you'll be using for the class.

I mention in the assignments that they are to do a paper and prepare a presentation. I usually try to get students to present their work. This is a good practice for what they will do in the business world. Most of the time, they will be required to prepare an analysis and present it. If you don't have the class time or inclination to have the students present, then you can of course cut out the aspect of them putting together a presentation.

If you want to point students toward highly ranked journals in AI, here's a list of the top journals as reported by *various citation counts sources* (this list changes year to year):

- Communications of the ACM
- Artificial Intelligence
- Cognitive Science
- IEEE Transactions on Pattern Analysis and Machine Intelligence
- Foundations and Trends in Machine Learning
- Journal of Memory and Language
- Cognitive Psychology
- Neural Networks
- IEEE Transactions on Neural Networks and Learning Systems
- IEEE Intelligent Systems
- Knowledge-based Systems

GUIDE TO USING THE CHAPTERS

For each of the chapters, I provide next some various ways to use the chapter material. You can assign the tasks as individual homework assignments, or the tasks can be used with team projects for the class. You can easily layout a series of assignments, such as indicating that the students are to do item "a" below for say Chapter 1, then "b" for the next chapter of the book, and so on.

a) What is the main point of the chapter and describe in your own words the significance of the topic,

b) Identify at least two aspects in the chapter that you agree with, and support your concurrence by providing at least one other outside researched item as support; make sure to explain your basis for disagreeing with the aspects,

c) Identify at least two aspects in the chapter that you disagree with, and support your disagreement by providing at least one other outside researched item as support; make sure to explain your basis for disagreeing with the aspects,

d) Find an aspect that was not covered in the chapter, doing so by conducting outside research, and then explain how that aspect ties into the chapter and what significance it brings to the topic,

e) Interview a specialist in industry about the topic of the chapter, collect from them their thoughts and opinions, and readdress the chapter by citing your source and how they compared and contrasted to the material,

f) Interview a relevant academic professor or researcher in a college or university about the topic of the chapter, collect from them their thoughts and opinions, and readdress the chapter by citing your source and how they compared and contrasted to the material,

g) Try to update a chapter by finding out the latest on the topic, and ascertain whether the issue or topic has now been solved or whether it is still being addressed, explain what you come up with.

The above are all ways in which you can get the students of your class involved in considering the material of a given chapter. You could mix things up by having one of those above assignments per each week, covering the chapters over the course of the semester or quarter.

As a reminder, here are the chapters of the book and you can select whichever chapters you find most valued for your particular class:

Chapter Title

1   Eliot Framework for AI Self-Driving Cars

2   Risk-O-Meters and AI Self-Driving Cars

3   Eroding Car Devotion and AI Self-Driving Cars

4   Drunk Driving Rises With Smart Cars

5   Driver's Difficulties and Smart Cars

6   Millennials Aren't As Car Crazed As Baby Boomers

7   Risks Of AI Self-Driving Cars

8   Major Phase Shift and AI Self-Driving Cars

9   Level 3 Tech Misgivings For Smart Cars

10   Presidential Debate Lessons and AI Self-Driving Cars

11   Cloud Breeches and AI Self-Driving Cars

12   The Moral Imperative and AI Self-Driving Cars

13   Freed Up Driver Time And AI Self-Driving Car

14   Deadliest Highways and AI Self-Driving Cars

15   Your Lyin' Eyes and AI Self-Driving Cars

16   Elon Musk Physics Mindset and AI Self-Driving Cars

Companion Book By This Author

Advances in AI and Autonomous Vehicles: Cybernetic Self-Driving Cars

Practical Advances in Artificial Intelligence (AI) and Machine Learning

by

Dr. Lance B. Eliot, MBA, PhD

This title is available via Amazon and other book sellers

Companion Book By This Author

Self-Driving Cars:
"The Mother of All AI Projects"

by Dr. Lance B. Eliot, MBA, PhD

This title is available via Amazon and other book sellers

Companion Book By This Author

Innovation and Thought Leadership
on Self-Driving Driverless Cars

by Dr. Lance B. Eliot, MBA, PhD

This title is available via Amazon and other book sellers

Companion Book By This Author

New Advances in AI Autonomous Driverless Cars Self-Driving Cars

by Dr. Lance B. Eliot, MBA, PhD

Chapter Title

This title is available via Amazon and other book sellers

Companion Book By This Author

Introduction to
Driverless Self-Driving Cars

by Dr. Lance B. Eliot, MBA, PhD

Chapter Title

This title is available via Amazon and other book sellers

This title is available via Amazon and other book sellers

Lance B. Eliot

Companion Book By This Author

Transformative Artificial Intelligence Driverless Self-Driving Cars

by Dr. Lance B. Eliot, MBA, PhD

This title is available via Amazon and other book sellers

Companion Book By This Author

Disruptive Artificial Intelligence and Driverless Self-Driving Cars

by Dr. Lance B. Eliot, MBA, PhD

Chapter Title

This title is available via Amazon and other book sellers

Companion Book By This Author

State-of-the-Art
AI Driverless Self-Driving Cars

by Dr. Lance B. Eliot, MBA, PhD

Chapter Title

This title is available via Amazon and other book sellers

Companion Book By This Author

Top Trends in
AI Self-Driving Cars

by Dr. Lance B. Eliot, MBA, PhD

This title is available via Amazon and other book sellers

Companion Book By This Author

AI Innovations
and Self-Driving Cars

by Dr. Lance B. Eliot, MBA, PhD

<u>Chapter Title</u>

This title is available via Amazon and other book sellers

Companion Book By This Author

Crucial Advances for
AI Self-Driving Cars

by Dr. Lance B. Eliot, MBA, PhD

This title is available via Amazon and other book sellers

Companion Book By This Author

Sociotechnical Insights and
AI Driverless Cars

by Dr. Lance B. Eliot, MBA, PhD

This title is available via Amazon and other book sellers

Companion Book By This Author

Pioneering Advances for AI Driverless Cars

by Dr. Lance B. Eliot, MBA, PhD

Chapter Title

This title is available via Amazon and other book sellers

This title is available via Amazon and other book sellers

Companion Book By This Author

The Cutting Edge of AI Autonomous Cars

by Dr. Lance B. Eliot, MBA, PhD

Chapter Title

This title is available via Amazon and other book sellers

Companion Book By This Author

The Next Wave of
AI Self-Driving Cars

by Dr. Lance B. Eliot, MBA, PhD

This title is available via Amazon and other book sellers

Companion Book By This Author

Revolutionary Innovations of
AI Self-Driving Cars

by Dr. Lance B. Eliot, MBA, PhD

Chapter Title

1 Eliot Framework for AI Self-Driving Cars

2 Exascale Supercomputer and AI Self-Driving Cars

3 Superhuman AI and AI Self-Driving Cars

4 Olfactory e-Nose Sensors and AI Self-Driving Cars

5 Perpetual Computing and AI Self-Driving Cars

6 Byzantine Generals Problem and AI Self-Driving Cars

7 Driver Traffic Guardians and AI Self-Driving Cars

8 Anti-Gridlock Laws and AI Self-Driving Cars

9 Arguing Machines and AI Self-Driving Cars

This title is available via Amazon and other book sellers

<u>Companion Book By This Author</u>

AI Self-Driving Cars
Breakthroughs

by Dr. Lance B. Eliot, MBA, PhD

This title is available via Amazon and other book sellers

Companion Book By This Author

Trailblazing Trends for AI Self-Driving Cars

by Dr. Lance B. Eliot, MBA, PhD

Chapter Title

This title is available via Amazon and other book sellers

Companion Book By This Author

Ingenious Strides for
AI Driverless Cars

by Dr. Lance B. Eliot, MBA, PhD

This title is available via Amazon and other book sellers

Companion Book By This Author

AI Self-Driving Cars
Inventiveness

by Dr. Lance B. Eliot, MBA, PhD

This title is available via Amazon and other book sellers

<u>Companion Book By This Author</u>

Visionary Secrets of
AI Driverless Cars

by Dr. Lance B. Eliot, MBA, PhD

<u>Chapter Title</u>

This title is available via Amazon and other book sellers

Companion Book By This Author

Spearheading
AI Self-Driving Cars

by Dr. Lance B. Eliot, MBA, PhD

Chapter Title

This title is available via Amazon and other book sellers

Companion Book By This Author

Spurring
AI Self-Driving Cars
by Dr. Lance B. Eliot, MBA, PhD

Chapter Title

This title is available via Amazon and other book sellers

Companion Book By This Author

Avant-Garde
AI Driverless Cars

by Dr. Lance B. Eliot, MBA, PhD

Chapter Title

This title is available via Amazon and other book sellers

Companion Book By This Author

AI Self-Driving Cars Evolvement

by Dr. Lance B. Eliot, MBA, PhD

This title is available via Amazon and other book sellers

Companion Book By This Author

AI Driverless Cars
Chrysalis
by Dr. Lance B. Eliot, MBA, PhD

Chapter Title

This title is available via Amazon and other book sellers

Companion Book By This Author

Boosting
AI Autonomous Cars
by Dr. Lance B. Eliot, MBA, PhD

<u>Chapter Title</u>

This title is available via Amazon and other book sellers

<u>Companion Book By This Author</u>

AI Self-Driving Cars Trendsetting

by Dr. Lance B. Eliot, MBA, PhD

<u>Chapter Title</u>

This title is available via Amazon and other book sellers

<u>Companion Book By This Author</u>

AI Autonomous Cars
Forefront

by Dr. Lance B. Eliot, MBA, PhD

<u>Chapter Title</u>

This title is available via Amazon and other book sellers

Companion Book By This Author

AI Autonomous Cars
Emergence

by Dr. Lance B. Eliot, MBA, PhD

Chapter Title

This title is available via Amazon and other book sellers

Companion Book By This Author

AI Autonomous Cars Progress

by Dr. Lance B. Eliot, MBA, PhD

This title is available via Amazon and other book sellers

Lance B. Eliot

ABOUT THE AUTHOR

Dr. Lance B. Eliot, MBA, PhD is the CEO of Techbruim, Inc. and Executive Director of the Cybernetic AI Self-Driving Car Institute, and has over twenty years of industry experience including serving as a corporate officer in a billion dollar firm and was a partner in a major executive services firm. He is also a serial entrepreneur having founded, ran, and sold several high-tech related businesses. He previously hosted the popular radio show *Technotrends* that was also available on American Airlines flights via their in-flight audio program. Author or co-author of a dozen books and over 400 articles, he has made appearances on CNN, and has been a frequent speaker at industry conferences.

A former professor at the University of Southern California (USC), he founded and led an innovative research lab on Artificial Intelligence in Business. Known as the "AI Insider" his writings on AI advances and trends has been widely read and cited. He also previously served on the faculty of the University of California Los Angeles (UCLA), and was a visiting professor at other major universities. He was elected to the International Board of the Society for Information Management (SIM), a prestigious association of over 3,000 high-tech executives worldwide.

He has performed extensive community service, including serving as Senior Science Adviser to the Vice Chair of the Congressional Committee on Science & Technology. He has served on the Board of the OC Science & Engineering Fair (OCSEF), where he is also has been a Grand Sweepstakes judge, and likewise served as a judge for the Intel International SEF (ISEF). He served as the Vice Chair of the Association for Computing Machinery (ACM) Chapter, a prestigious association of computer scientists. Dr. Eliot has been a shark tank judge for the USC Mark Stevens Center for Innovation on start-up pitch competitions, and served as a mentor for several incubators and accelerators in Silicon Valley and Silicon Beach. He served on several Boards and Committees at USC, including having served on the Marshall Alumni Association (MAA) Board in Southern California.

Dr. Eliot holds a PhD from USC, MBA, and Bachelor's in Computer Science, and earned the CDP, CCP, CSP, CDE, and CISA certifications. Born and raised in Southern California, and having traveled and lived internationally, he enjoys scuba diving, surfing, and sailing.

ADDENDUM

AI Autonomous Cars Progress

Practical Advances in Artificial Intelligence (AI)
and Machine Learning

By
Dr. Lance B. Eliot, MBA, PhD

———

For supplemental materials of this book, visit:

www.ai-selfdriving-cars.guru

For special orders of this book, contact:
LBE Press Publishing
Email: LBE.Press.Publishing@gmail.com

www.ingramcontent.com/pod-product-compliance
Lightning Source LLC
Chambersburg PA
CBHW051046050326
40690CB00006B/618